Quarterly Essay

1   THE WHITE QUEEN
One Nation and the Politics of Race
David Marr

103   CORRESPONDENCE
Jacinta Nampijinpa Price, Amy McQuire, George Megalogenis,
Marcia Langton, Kim Mahood, Jon Altman, Nicholas Biddle, Stan Grant

139   Contributors

Quarterly Essay is published four times a year by Black Inc., an imprint of Schwartz Publishing Pty Ltd. Publisher: Morry Schwartz.

ISBN 978-1-86395-907-0 ISSN 1832-0953

Subscriptions − 1 year print & digital (4 issues): $79.95 within Australia incl. GST. Outside Australia $119.95. 2 years print & digital (8 issues): $149.95 within Australia incl. GST. 1 year digital only: $39.95.

Payment may be made by Mastercard or Visa, or by cheque made out to Schwartz Publishing. Payment includes postage and handling.

To subscribe, fill out and post the subscription card or form inside this issue, or subscribe online:

www.quarterlyessay.com
subscribe@blackincbooks.com
Phone: 61 3 9486 0288

Correspondence should be addressed to:

The Editor, Quarterly Essay
Level 1, 221 Drummond Street
Carlton VIC 3053 Australia
Phone: 61 3 9486 0288 / Fax: 61 3 9011 6106
Email: quarterlyessay@blackincbooks.com

Editor: Chris Feik. Management: Caitlin Yates. Publicity: Anna Lensky. Design: Guy Mirabella. Assistant Editor: Kirstie Innes-Will. Production Coordinator: Hanako Smith. Typesetting: Tristan Main.

Printed in Australia by McPherson's Printing Group. The paper used to produce this book comes from wood grown in sustainable forests.

THE WHITE QUEEN

One Nation and the Politics of Race

David Marr

RANGA REDUX

One afternoon last November, Pauline Hanson stood under threatening Canberra skies and cracked a bottle of bubbles to celebrate the victory of Donald Trump. She was beside herself with excitement. Words tumbled out of her:

> Hi, everyone. We're out the front of Parliament House, Canberra, Australia, and why we are here – well, I'm so excited that Donald Trump looks like he's just over the line and I'm so happy about it because this is putting out a clear message to everyone around the world that the people power is now happening and it's happened in Australia.

Emotions cross Hanson's face like storms over a desert. The prevailing weather is petulance but she shows delight vividly. Her eyes flash and that tight red mouth breaks into a winning grin. Love or loathe this woman, you can always tell what she's thinking. On the afternoon of Trump's victory, Hanson's face registered vindication, glee and such breathless pleasure she seemed to be claiming a hand in his triumph. Flanked by one of her senators, she toasted the president to be, the American people ("Good on you, guys"), Brexit and the triumphant return of One Nation to Canberra. "It's all about people power," she declared, raising her glass of Black Pig. "And I'm so happy."

The return of Pauline Hanson calls for national reflection. A strange gap has opened between the mood of this country and the temper of its politics. The decent Australia revealed in poll after poll seems not to be the country our politicians are representing. Most Australians reject everything Hanson stands for, but politics in this country has been orbiting around One Nation since the day she returned to Canberra. The lesson from her poor showing in Western Australia is that this doesn't have to be. Yet politicians are showing little more enthusiasm in its aftermath for doing what needs to be done: tackling Hanson head-on. They know it's a risky strategy: she's durable and Turnbull can barely govern without her block of senators behind him.

This woman went to prison, danced the cha-cha on national television for a couple of years, and failed so often at the ballot box she became a running joke. But the truth is she never left us. She was always knocking on the door. Most of those defeats at the polls were close-run things. For twenty years political leaders appeased Hanson's followers while working to keep her out of office. The first strategy tainted Australian politics. The second eventually failed. So she's with us again – the Kabuki make-up, that mop of red hair and the voice telling us what we already know: "I'm fed up." The years show. So does the determination etched into her face. She doesn't rant as much these days. "She's got the art of the soundbite down," says Simon Hunt, who dogged her last time as the monstrous Pauline Pantsdown. He's watching and waiting to see if he will pounce again. He rates her better with the camera now, better at laughing off hostile questions, better at switching the topic, better at filling the gaps when her sentences break down. "She's just another politician." But six or seven years on *Sunrise* haven't touched her voice. "It says 'You're just like us, Pauline.'" And the damage of the years? Hunt hesitates. "Remember back then when she said one time: 'I am the mother of the nation'? Maybe she is now."

This is an Australian story. Positioning herself as the local leader of an international uprising is a wild boast. She commands nothing like the numbers backing Trump and the Brexit leader Nigel Farage and the daughter of the French far right Marine Le Pen. Compared to them, Hanson is a bit player. And this is a better country. No swathe of Australia was destroyed by the global financial crisis. Most of us don't share the toxic fears of immigration driving the United Kingdom out of Europe. Even so, public discourse has focused since her return on globalisation, the death of manufacturing, wages growth, inequality, grim prospects in little towns and the nation's exasperation with politics. Those issues aren't irrelevant, but we are not facing the facts about Hanson and One Nation. What's driving them is the same as last time: race.

Aborigines are forgotten. Asians are old hat. These days Hanson targets Muslims, and that brought her over the line in 2016. She was on the hustings in Western Australia in January this year when a crazed man drove his car into an afternoon crowd in Melbourne. The bodies were still being cleared away when her adviser, James Ashby, whispered a couple of words into her ear and she turned to the camera with a look of a woman whose point had been proved. "I've just been told there's a terrorist attack that's just happened in Melbourne," she said, before venting her fury on Muslims. "People don't look right. That they are not going to assimilate into our society. How they have different ideology, different beliefs, don't abide by our laws, our culture, our way of life. Don't let them in! Make this country safe for its future generations!" But there was no terrorist link. The accused driver is from a Greek-Australian family. Hanson's words were deplored on television that night as hasty and clumsy and hard. But no one said bluntly what she was up to: race-baiting.

She's no fool, but it's not a big intelligence. She's learnt hard lessons along the way that make her a more formidable politician now than she was in the late 1990s. But only a prime minister desperate for her Senate votes would say of One Nation as Malcolm Turnbull has: "It is not a single issue party or a single personality party." He's dead wrong on both counts. Hanson is what she's always been: a white woman speaking for old white Australia. She hasn't changed. Nor has her party. But Australia has: we have come to accommodate her. When the Member for Oxley appeared in Canberra twenty years ago, the headlines were tough:

RACIST JIBES NO STUMBLING BLOCK
RACISM THE WORST PART OF ELECTION
RACISM IN POLITICS
RACISM THE UGLY EXPRESSION OF HUMANITY'S TRIBAL URGE
HANSON STANDS BY RACE VIEWS

We don't see such headlines now. Back in those days she was seen as an aberration. Not anymore. A great part of her allure then was the figure she cut before angry crowds: a slight woman, often rattled, finding the courage to speak her mind in the face of hostile demonstrations. The angry crowds have gone. These days she seems hardly even a surprise. She was such big news in Asia the first time around that the Foreign Press Association declared her the most famous Australian in the world. These days she makes no headlines offshore. In the late 1990s she had a life expectancy on the national stage of no more than a couple of years. This time she's won a place in the Senate for six and brought a knot of senators with her. Old enemies are now all smiles. Tony Abbott calls her "a voice of responsibility." Forgotten these days are the words of Liberal grandees led by Malcolm Fraser, who denounced her at her debut:

Racist politics are evil. Through the centuries men and women have suffered because they were presumed to be different from other people in their communities. Such people have been exploited, they have been killed, they have been "ethnically cleansed." Such barbarism continues even today in the Balkans. No decent community can compromise with racist policies. There is only one honourable option: absolute rejection, refusal to cooperate, refusal to lend credibility to those promoting the evil of racism.

Fraser was a figure from another time, already in parliament when it became clear in the early 1960s that unless we ditched the White Australia policy this country would become an international pariah. Most Australians wanted this done. Even so, dismantling the old race-based immigration scheme was politically hazardous and took time. At each step of the way it was understood on both sides of politics that they would not play to the minority angry – often bitterly angry – at the prospect of Australia being opened to other races and other faiths. The votes out there would not be exploited. That political truce survived seven prime ministers, from Holt to Hawke, two or three recessions and the arrival of 100,000 refugees from Vietnam before it was repudiated by John Howard. So began the modern politics of race in Canberra.

Howard has a maxim: "Politics is relentlessly driven by the laws of arithmetic." It sounds so simple, as if democracy ticks over almost of its own accord. But in the hands of a master like Howard, electoral mathematics is no simple exercise. What set him apart in the late 1990s was his eagerness to hunt for small pockets of votes out on the fringe where Hanson had her following. Many Australians look on the fears that drive those votes as an embarrassment, but for ruthlessly professional politicians they are a valuable resource. Gathering them took subtlety once. Howard was the great dog-whistler, the politician who could send a signal to the bush that went almost unheard in town. And Australia's voting system – we have to turn up and tick every box on ballots for the lower house – means national elections can be won or lost on tiny swings in marginal seats. Hanson stormed Canberra last year with a national Senate vote of 4.3 per cent. Though her support has seesawed in the states, her national following as this essay goes to press is holding at 9 per cent. With the two-party system fraying at its edges and a great brawl for votes out on the right, this has been enough for Hanson to have an extraordinary impact on this country: an outlier skewing national politics her way. The arithmetic that entangles Australia in the race fears of country towns and the outer suburbs in 2017 is the struggle on both sides of politics for Hanson's few per cent.

Hanson didn't create her constituency but when she is around, contest for these votes is fierce. That's what makes her a political star: she breaks down allegiances. She shifts votes around the map. If One Nation flames out again in bickering and feuds as it did the last time, parties big and little will be there to hoover up her vote. They are already positioning themselves. The Coalition is after them. Ditto Labor. The Nationals will fight as they did twenty years ago for every last vote Hanson has filched from them. She is, after all, what the bush most deplores: competition.

But Hanson's people can't be easily bought off. I'll come to the fine detail later but, in broad brush, One Nation voters in 2016 were absolutely Australian: the Aussie children of Aussie parents. They identify as proudly working class. They aren't dying out: roughly a third of those who voted for Hanson last year were under forty-five. Despite its reputation as a bush party, half One Nation's strength lies in big cities. Almost all Hanson's voters left school early but went on to make a good fist of their lives. She is typical of her kind: out at fifteen and a prosperous woman by forty. Her followers aren't poor or unemployed. One Nation was very much a man's party in the early days but now many more women are backing Hanson. There's not a whiff of faith-based moralising about One Nation. It's a rare Hanson voter who ever darkens the doors of a church. These people are secular, working-class conservatives who see eye to eye on a short list of big issues.

First is their affection for her. It's not uncritical. Hanson's voters can see she's often outlandish, indeed way out of line, yet brave and speaking for them. One Nation is her following. Without Hanson there is no party.

Second is their deep disenchantment with politics. Australians are disgruntled with government. The figures are alarming. The 2016 Australian

Election Study found 74 per cent of us believe governments look after themselves rather than doing the right thing by all of us. (Much more of the AES later.) While most Australians are disgruntled, the One Nation constituency is furious. Among Hanson's people it is an article of faith that government isn't delivering for them. The system is set against them. No one is speaking for them. No one is listening.

Third is their fierce nostalgia. Many of us wish Australia was still the country of our childhoods. We don't long for lost greatness. That's an American thing. But most of us at some time have wished this was still the familiar country we first knew. What sets One Nation voters apart is their wish to go back there, even if it meant living a poorer life. The money doesn't matter. They want to go back to a country that had factories and tariffs and a sure place for them – a country that was white. And they feel the loss of this Australia fiercely.

Fourth is their profound hostility to that great agent of change, immigration. Other articles of faith for Hanson voters are that the intake must be cut dramatically; that immigrants bring crime and take our jobs; and that immigration does this country little good. Australians are uniquely hostile to boat people, but One Nation voters are twice as likely as the rest of us to demand that every last refugee boat be sent back out to sea.

Fifth is the driver of race. Ever since Hanson first appeared on the scene, analysts have wondered whether she runs a party of protest or a party of policy. I'll get to that illuminating dispute later. But on whatever reading of Hanson, race is strongly in the mix. Yet neither Coalition nor Labor leader will bluntly call Hanson on race as she demands an end to Muslim immigration; surveillance cameras in mosques; halal certification and all face coverings to be banned; and a royal commission into the truth behind the masquerade of Islam posing as a religion. This is heavy-duty stuff, but the tactical impulse of the major parties is to flinch from naming her for what she is. In the face of her rants they make formal declarations deploring attacks on Muslims. They boast the great success of multiculturalism in this country. Turnbull can hold an Iftar dinner at

Kirribilli House – he may not hold another – but both Liberal and Labor leaders are reluctant to call her directly on race. They both balk at the task. "People in politics cannot say, 'Madam, you are a racist,' because too many swinging voters are racist," a Labor insider in Queensland told me. "We need their votes. If you're calling Pauline a racist, what those people are hearing is, you're calling me a racist."

We can't go back to the White Australia policy. It's impossible to ban Muslim immigration. We can't rebuild tariff walls. Much of the time all government can offer Hanson's voters are consolation prizes. That's happening now: more pork for bush electorates; stiffer citizenship tests; new cruelties for boat people; fresh barriers for Chinese investment; the prospect of more coal-fired power stations dotting the landscape; and giving at least a sympathetic ear to calls for hate speech to be let loose by gutting the *Racial Discrimination Act*. Turnbull is being held to the pact he made with the National Party when he overthrew Abbott: bush pork (again), a promise never to introduce carbon pricing or emissions trading while he remains prime minister, and a pledge to hold a plebiscite before legalising equal marriage. It's hardly the agenda of modern Australia. The pact is pure One Nation.

For twenty years the Liberals refused to do deals with Hanson as elections rolled around. They tried it once in the early days and learnt what damage she does to the Liberal brand. But in Western Australia earlier this year, with Colin Barnett's government in extremis, a preference deal was done with One Nation. Liberals said soothing words about Hanson's new maturity, depth and skill. Jeff Kennett, who once publicly implored Howard not to do such a deal, supported this one. As he explained to me, Hanson's views on race are not what matter now. "Pauline Hanson's group has actually assisted the government in getting through some difficult legislation, right?" The deal backfired. Barnett was tainted. Hanson's polling figures fell away from the moment it was announced. The anti-politician politician was exposed backing the Liberals. Her big victory evaporated. In the end she won only 8 per cent of the vote in the seats One Nation contested. She said next day: "Doing the deal with the Libs has done damage to us, in all honesty. It was a mistake." Labor was left to enjoy a mighty victory.

Memories of her crashing and burning when she first appeared in Canberra were a big comfort for those appalled to see her back again in 2017. For a time back then she had looked to be an unstoppable force. Then it all fell apart. But despite this fiasco in Western Australia, Hanson is looking more durable this time around. Come what may, she is in the Senate for six years. Her people aren't going anywhere. She's a character. Time and again Australians forgive her blunders.

Since returning to Canberra she has survived a purge at party headquarters and the buffoonish behaviour of her one-time senator Rod Culleton. When trouble broke over his head, she took a hard look at the man and walked away. She was called a traitor in the party but this was the right call taken by a woman determined to last. The one lesson she seems to have brought back from the wilderness is the need for her to be in absolute command. Some weeks before the poll, when her candidates in Western Australia were growing restive, Hanson went on television to deliver a message to them, her party and the nation. It was delivered with terrifying certainty:

> If you're not prepared to follow direction, then please, I suggest, that you walk away from the party – you stand as an independent – because you will not be welcome. I will not have this dissension now. They chose to join One Nation. They've chosen to stand as a candidate, and we are a united team. If they're not prepared to actually do that, well then, I suggest that they go and stand as an independent and because I'm not going to have this. I want a strong, united team. Follow directions from, you know, the party, as such. And that's what the people want. They want clear, precise direction. I've got a lot to do for the people in this country.

Peter Scanlon was just a kid in the early 1950s when he worked behind the counter in his father's newsagency in the Melbourne suburb of Coburg, which was full of Italian and Greek migrants. "Every morning they were coming in getting their newspaper on the way to work. Dad was a great explainer of how much courage these people had shown to come here and start a life. So that was bred in me from an early age. He made us share time with these people, be patient with their language and interested in their different cultures. All those things that were strange to most of us at that stage, Dad embraced and taught each of us kids that we needed to embrace – and with some vigour I might add. If you sniggered at someone who couldn't get their tenses right in English when they ordered a paper, you got a clip behind the ear for not understanding how tough it was for them."

After making his pile with Patrick Corporation, Scanlon set up a foundation in 2000 and began researching Australian attitudes to immigration because he discovered there was so little good data about what he sees as the most defining feature of Australia: the settlement of migrants in large numbers. "What I could see was struggles when I was growing up to settle other Europeans who couldn't speak English and who were from Christian-based countries. Our migration was changing to non-Europeans and non-Christians. And I wasn't sure we had done enough work to help existing Australians understand how to cope." It was the same struggle he had watched as a kid: "But bigger and tougher."

The foundation's first national survey, conducted by Andrew Markus of Monash University, appeared in 2007. Markus was analysing the way race works in the politics of this country long before Pauline Hanson appeared on the scene. For this essay I've drawn heavily on his 2001 book, *Race: John Howard and the Remaking of Australia*. A precise man with a worried gaze, Markus pins everything to numbers, and the numbers he's gathered over nine "Mapping Social Cohesion" surveys are huge: 16,000 of us have been questioned in half a dozen languages about our attitudes to race, immigration and Australian society. The latest survey, conducted in the weeks immediately after the 2016 election, is a snapshot of the nation that gave us back Malcolm Turnbull and Pauline Hanson.

The good numbers are so good. Here is fresh proof we live in an open, orderly, optimistic and tolerant society. We love this place. We're not blind to its faults and we want them addressed. We worry about the poor. Inequality distresses us. The power of big business makes us uneasy. The nation is settling down with *Wik* and *Mabo*. And our door is wide open to the world. We are curious about new people and their ways. More than almost any people on earth, we are happy for migrants to come in big numbers. Families from Asia are almost as welcome here as families from Europe. But once again the survey lays bare the grim minorities. Hanson is a creature of these minorities. These numbers map the Australia where race politics are played. First the good news:

Australians are happy with their lot. A steady 85 per cent or more of us report the year just past was a happy one. Three-quarters of us are satisfied, in particular, with our financial situation. Neither the GFC nor the end of the mining boom has shaken the confidence of nearly all of us that the good fortune of the country will continue. As for our own and our children's futures: 80 per cent of us believe we live in a land of economic opportunity where hard work brings a better life.

'Australia is a land of economic opportunity where in the long run, hard work brings a better life', 2007-2016

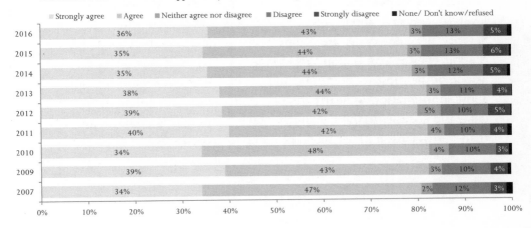

■ Strongly agree ■ Agree ■ Neither agree nor disagree ■ Disagree ■ Strongly disagree ■ None/ Don't know/refused

Year	Strongly agree	Agree	Neither	Disagree	Strongly disagree	None/Don't know/refused
2016	36%	43%	3%	13%	5%	
2015	35%	44%	3%	13%	6%	
2014	35%	44%	3%	12%	5%	
2013	38%	44%	3%	11%	4%	
2012	39%	42%	5%	10%	5%	
2011	40%	42%	4%	10%	4%	
2010	34%	48%	4%	10%	3%	
2009	39%	43%	3%	10%	4%	
2007	34%	47%	2%	12%	3%	

Australians are committed to their country. Though we are a new people – more than a quarter of us were born abroad and another quarter have at least one parent born abroad – there is nothing in the Scanlon surveys to show we're losing our sense of being Australian. We don't see ourselves as a nation riven by division. From the start, the Scanlon surveys have shown over 90 per cent of us feel we belong in this place.

'To what extent do you have a sense of belonging in Australia?', 2007-2016

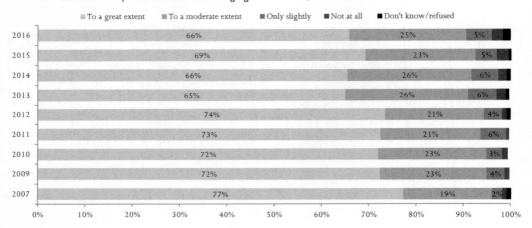

Australians welcome mass immigration. The 2016 survey recorded the lowest level of concern about migrant numbers since these surveys began. Seventy per cent of us are happy with them or want them increased. Markus cites a 2014 Gallup World Poll as evidence of Australia's position as one of the most welcoming countries in the world. Britain is in a fever about immigration – nearly 70 per cent there want migrant numbers cut – and hostility to the size of the intake is far higher in the United States than here. Hanson hasn't much of a Brexit/Trump wave to ride.

Attitudes towards immigration: Top 10 migrant destination countries (%)

In your view, should immigration in this country be kept at its present level, increased or decreased?

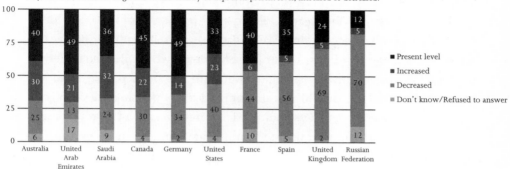

- Present level
- Increased
- Decreased
- Don't know/Refused to answer

We don't want refugees coming here by boat. The Scanlon survey confirms the findings of so many others that there's a powerful majority — a very Australian majority — hostile to boat people. In 2016, 61 per cent of those quizzed by the Scanlon teams disapproved of asylum seekers trying to make their way here by boat and a third wanted them pushed back out to sea.

'Which of the following four statements comes closest to your view about the best policy for dealing with asylum seekers trying to reach Australia by boat?', 2010-2015

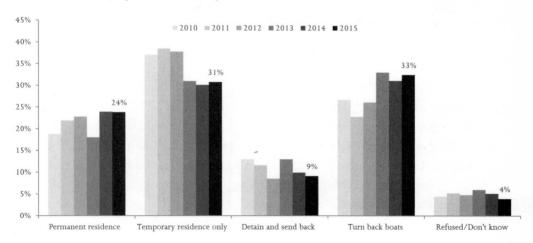

Multiculturalism is a popular triumph. Hardly anyone barracks for assimilation anymore. Multiculturalism is a very strong brand. Markus has been interrogating these figures for years: "Eighty-five per cent of people think multiculturalism is a good thing. We've had five goes at that over five years and it's hard to get that figure under 75 per cent anywhere. But the underlying thing is that, nonetheless, multiculturalism for most people is about integration. It's not like the old assimilationist idea that people once simplistically accepted. But nonetheless they look for integration, and groups they perceive as not integrating concern them. Integration does mean eventually you don't wear head covering."

'Multiculturalism has been good for Australia', 2013-2016

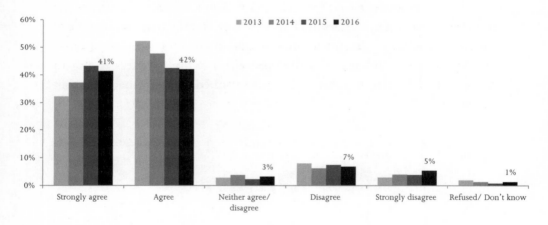

We know Australia is stronger for its many races and many faiths. The Scanlon polls have shown this for a decade, and a world survey conducted in 2016 by the US Pew Research Center puts Australia in a leading position. Pew asked: "Overall, do you think having an increasing number of people of many different races, ethnic groups and nationalities makes your country a better or a worse place to live?" Better:

Italy	18 per cent
Germany	26 per cent
France	26 per cent
UK	33 per cent
Australia	49 per cent

The dark materials. "What makes Australia unique is its acceptance of immigration and cultural diversity," says Markus. But that's not the whole picture. "On the basis of Scanlon Foundation polling and a number of additional surveys conducted over the last thirty years, there is support for the conclusion that the core level of intolerance in Australia is close to 10 per cent of the population. Using a broader definition (incorporating both the strongest negative and next negative response), levels of intolerance and rejection of cultural diversity are probably in the range 25 to 30 per cent of the population." Each year, lately, he has seen signs of deterioration. "We're measuring more strong negatives." In the 2016 survey he reported "emerging signs of increased pessimism, relatively high levels of negativity towards Muslims and an increase in the proportion of people experiencing discrimination on the basis of skin colour, ethnicity or religion."

Discrimination. Complaints of discrimination were higher in 2016 than at any time since the Scanlon surveys began. Some reported physical abuse and property damage. Others felt unfairly denied jobs or promotion. The most common complaint was verbal abuse. The young fared worse than the old. The blacker you are, the higher the risk of discrimination. In their 2016 report *Australians Today*, the Scanlon teams found discrimination had been experienced that year by:

    39 per cent of people born in India
    39 per cent born in China
    55 per cent born in South Korea
    67 per cent born in Kenya
    75 per cent born in Zimbabwe
    77 per cent born in South Sudan

Muslims. Markus found a record 14 per cent of Australians admitting to "very negative" attitudes to Muslims in 2016, plus another 10 per cent of us having "somewhat negative" feelings. All in all, a quarter of the country is feeling disturbed to some degree by the Muslim 2 per cent of the population. In the experience of the Scanlon surveys, the terms "Muslim" and "Middle Eastern" are virtually interchangeable.

'Is your personal attitude positive, negative or neutral towards Muslims?', Scanlon Foundation surveys 2010-2016

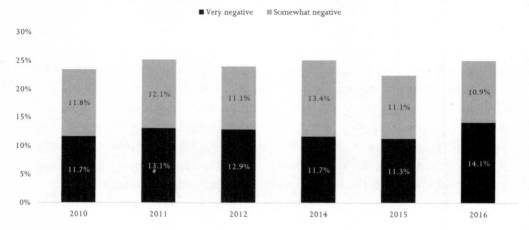

Other polls have even more alarming figures. In September 2016, Essential reported 49 per cent of Australians wanted an end to all Muslim immigration. The news caused a sensation. Other pollsters were sceptical. At issue here are the "commercial panels" used by Essential – respondents recruited by competitions, opt-in, through email lists, and so on – rather than fresh random samples. In October, Roy Morgan Research published a poll showing majority support (58 per cent to 33 per cent) for Muslim immigration. A small sample of One Nation voters indicated hostility among Hanson's people to Muslims settling in Australia is tracking at 87 per cent.

Markus ran some numbers to let me sketch a group portrait of those 25 per cent of us troubled by Islam. Half of them are over sixty-five. The usual rule applies: more education, less fear. A third of those who never finished school have negative feelings towards Muslims compared to 18 per cent of Australians with university degrees. These people aren't knuckle-draggers. Like the rest of us, they want social change – almost all of them want to see euthanasia and medical marijuana legalised – and they are exasperated with Canberra. The more hostile Australians are to Muslims, the more they want the system of government in this country changed radically or even replaced.

But the sharpest focus of their hostility is, of course, on immigration: those of us with negative feelings towards Muslims are twice as likely to object to the size of the intake (66 per cent compared to 34 per cent for Australians as a whole) and to be unconvinced that bringing people in from many different countries and cultures makes Australia stronger (41 per cent compared to 67 per cent). Their attitudes to boat people are particularly ferocious, with 85 per cent of them disapproving of refugees trying to make their way here under their own steam.

Hostility to Muslims is driving these voters away from the major parties. When asked how they intended to vote:

9 per cent said for the Greens
23 per cent said for Labor
27 per cent said for the Coalition
38 per cent said for independents

This territory is Hanson's hunting ground.

What does Scanlon think of the Australia his foundation is mapping? "On the good side, I'm staggered how resilient we have been accepting the change in the source of our migrants. We've done a lot better at that than I thought we may have. I am disappointed by the older age group in Australia, particularly those living in regional areas where there are no migrants. It is an amazing fact to me that the most blowback we get is from people who don't have any experience with them!" He's not shocked by the 25 per cent chunk hostile to Muslims. "You have 10 to 15 per cent hardcore you'll never change, and the rest can be manipulated by Pauline Hanson. That's enough to have a big impact on government. The sad part about our current democracy is that the two major parties can't work out they will die if they don't work together. What they're doing is allowing the fringe to take control." He is sure things will turn out as well for Iraqi Muslims as they did for Greeks and Italians. But how long will it take? "Twenty-five years. It'll be their kids." And beyond that? "The degree of difficulty of proper settlement is exaggerated when there are key physical differences. Being black at the moment is significantly different."

By the time John Howard was once again leader of the Opposition, Pauline Hanson was in the last weeks of a short career as an Ipswich city councillor. "She wasn't given much time to distinguish herself," David Leser wrote in a celebrated profile: "In her brief time on council she gave clues to her eventual tub-thumping on race. She opposed an Aboriginal kindergarten on the grounds that there were already enough kindergartens in the area." She got into the game when a new man in her life, Rick Gluyas, persuaded her to run for council. Ipswich was a Labor citadel. He was part of a local revolt against party bosses in Brisbane. Hanson was one of a bunch of independents who seized control of the city for a couple of years before the party fought back. Fresh elections were called and she was narrowly defeated in March 1995. A pattern was set. She wrote:

> I lost my seat by 132 primary votes ... I had no chance with the boundary changes to my electorate and the preference deals they had done with nearly all the candidates putting me last on their how-to-vote cards. It gave me my first taste of things to come ... I should have woken up then to the devious and dirty game of politics!

In truth, she had found her calling. She was hungry for attention, relished campaigning and, having whipped her business into shape, believed Australia could use her brand of militant common sense:

> The majority of politicians, as far as I was concerned, had no idea about job security, running a business or employing staff. Unions were holding the country to ransom, equality was out the window and political correctness was being forced upon us.

She wanted another go. Late in 1995 she offered herself as a Liberal candidate for the federal seat of Oxley. Elections were due sometime the following year. No one gave her a chance. Hanson was chosen as a presentable loser. "She was a good bit of gear at the beginning of the race," the local party leader Steve Wilson told Leser. "She was a small business-woman who worked hard, had had her fair share of knocks and had a genuine concern for the people. A classic Liberal ... she was pick of the bunch."

She was forty-one, twice divorced and the mother of four children. Cafés were the family's trade. Her parents ran a famous hamburger joint in Brisbane near the Gabba. "If you want anything in life, you have to work for it," was the lesson Hanson took from her parents' success. "Nobody owes you anything." In the late 1980s she bought Marsden's Seafood in the suburb of Ipswich. She never liked seafood but she was always good with money. By the time she started dabbling in politics, she had five staff and the shop was open seven days a week. She had an invest-ment property in town and had just built her dream home on a bare hill outside the city, where she ran a few head of cattle and Arabian mares. Her youngest son went to Ipswich Grammar. Despite that trademark voice, she was no scrubber, but fit, prosperous and itching for a fight.

Ipswich was a seedy town south of Brisbane, an ordinary place she was about to make famous. A couple of mines were working and coal was still being barged down the river to Brisbane. But government was the big employer in town, at the Railway Workshops and the Amberley RAAF base. Life was peaceful enough, but for as long as anyone could remember there had been friction between blacks and whites in the streets and schools. Aboriginals and Islanders lived mainly in public housing – not least because it was difficult to find landlords who would rent to them – and though they made up only a couple of per cent of the population, they were seen as the cause of all petty crime in town. Hanson was not alone in resenting the appearance of an Aboriginal legal service and health service in Ipswich. Nor was she out of step with the town – or Queensland – in thinking land rights for blacks had gone way too far. *Mabo* was a mystery. The long-running Royal Commission into Aboriginal Deaths in Custody had seemed to end by offering black pris-oners an escape from the punishment they deserved. Urban myths flourished. Debra Jopson, exploring the town for the *Sydney Morning Herald*, came across a local solicitor called Paul Fallu, whose family had lived in Ipswich for the best part of a century. He spoke of local misconceptions set hard:

> Fallu cannot convince one elderly woman that the Federal Government does not pay Aborigines the taxi fare to pick up their social security payments ... Another popular myth was that the Queensland Department of Aboriginal and Islander Affairs picked up the tab for Aborigines who defaulted on car loans ... Fallu and others claimed local media concentrated on the handful of Aboriginal juvenile delinquents shoplifting, harassing people and breaking-and-entering, virtually ignoring their non-Aboriginal counterparts.

Hanson worked on instinct. She made no secret of this. Hers was knowledge picked up over the counter and from the pages of the local rag, the *Queensland Times*. It wasn't a passion for politics but an affair – now ended – that had taken her to the city council. Politics was no more than an interest. She wrote: "I loved political discussions and often had them with friends, customers and neighbours." It wasn't until television cameras began to circle that she hired someone to dig out a few facts and figures to use.

> I had no documentation, no statistics and no research. I was just armed with the knowledge from talking to countless other Australians over the years, people who were also fed up with the whole Aboriginal issue and the waste of taxpayers' dollars.

Her ignorance had this advantage: she came to politics without baggage. Hanson wasn't a daughter of the lunatic fringe. She was neither nakedly paranoid nor preaching the anti-Semitic gospel of the League of Rights. Her background was a shop and a council. She had the endorsement of the Liberal Party.

On New Year's Day 1996, a young black prisoner in Townsville was found hanging from a length of rope in his cell. Fifteen black prisoners had died in Queensland in the previous year. This fresh death in the north led Indigenous leaders to threaten action at the United Nations. A despairing Robert Tickner, Minister for Aboriginal and Torres Strait Islander Affairs in Paul Keating's government, urged Queensland to implement the royal commission's recommendations. Hanson picked up her pen. The famous letter she wrote to the local paper reads like a first rough draft of the speeches John Howard would soon be delivering:

> Black deaths in custody seem to be Robert Tickner's latest outcry. Pity that as much media coverage or political grandstanding is not shown for white deaths in custody. As for Tickner's statement that Aborigines should not go to jail because apparently it is not working: imagine what type of country this would be to live if Aborigines didn't go to jail for their crimes. One of these men was serving a 12-year sentence and it wasn't just a speeding fine.
>
> Can you imagine then if we had equality, then we would have no prisoners at all. The indigenous people of this country are as much responsible for their actions as any other colour or race in this country. The problem is that politicians in all their profound wisdom have and are causing a racism problem.
>
> I would be the first to admit that, not that many years ago the Aborigines were treated wrongly but in trying to correct this they have gone too far. I don't feel responsible for the treatment of Aboriginal people in the past because I had no say but my concern now is for the future. How can you expect this race to help themselves when government showers them with money, facilities and opportunities that only these people can obtain no matter how minute the indigenous blood that is flowing through their veins, and this is what is causing racism. Until government wake up to themselves and start looking at equality not colour then we might start to work together as one.

The kerfuffle this caused died down after a few days when the Liberal Party apologised for her "calculated and callous attack" on Aborigines. That should have been that. But a few days after Keating called the election, Hanson got word that black demonstrators were descending on Marsden's Seafoods. She rushed to the shop and rang the *Queensland Times*. "I will not back down," she screamed. "I will not be dictated to by this group." When challenged, Hanson doubles down. She didn't think for a moment about the Liberal Party. Her firecracker pride exploded all over the pages of the local paper. At this point, her Labor opponents badly miscalculated. They saw Hanson's outburst as a gift from the gods and alerted the Brisbane press to the latest misbehaviour of the wild Liberal in Ipswich. Hanson then gave a fresh blast to the *Courier-Mail*. She was summoned to Brisbane by the party that afternoon and sacked on John Howard's orders. That confrontation came to have mythic significance for Hanson. It's the moment she always cites when asked how she came to choose her path in politics. As she tells it, "It was like being told, 'Hey, listen, you know nothing, we know everything, you shut up and we'll tell you what to do." Driving home to Ipswich she decided to fight the last fortnight of the campaign as an independent.

By the time Howard had come to parliament, his only faith was politics. But he was a keen Methodist in his youth and his views on race came to him then with the force of religious conviction. "Missions were very much part of the Methodist Church," he told me when I discussed this with him in his early years as prime minister. "It was very much a Christian mission to assist, so it was thought, people towards a better life." Methodists believed in assimilation. They taught their charges in the north and out in the Pacific a Western way of life. Howard looked back on this teaching as perhaps misguided but not racist. "People at that time acted out of the best of motives." Methodist kids weren't taught that the Aboriginal people were dispossessed or that whites might have an obligation to make restitution. "It was not a matter of debate." Howard would always insist that the Stolen Generations were too far past for people of his generation to bear any responsibility. But when he was turning out for church in the Sydney suburbs, the Methodists were still in the business of taking Aboriginal children from their families. It would go on for another decade before, appalled by their own record, they became leaders in a push for redress, justice and respect for Aboriginal rights. But Howard had moved away from his old church by then, leaving him, as Sir Alan Walker, the patriarch of Australian Methodism, judged, "stalled in his old attitudes."

As Malcolm Fraser's young treasurer, Howard never contested the programs of the Fraser government: land rights, an Aboriginal Development Corporation and a capital fund to compensate for the dispossession of traditional lands. Fraser's Minister for Aboriginal Affairs, Ian Viner, told me: "Howard showed no interest in land rights or Aboriginal matters." Without complaint, he signed the cheques. Fraser gave vast tracts of land in the Northern Territory to Aborigines, and Bob Hawke was elected promising to do the same in Western Australia. But then, in 1985, Howard became leader of the Opposition.

Mining companies were pouring a fortune into a ruthlessly executed campaign to block the extension of land rights. It was driven by Western Mining's Hugh Morgan, who roamed Australia preaching the perils of Aboriginal "sovereignty"; the religious mission of the mining industry; the heroism of white settlement; and the barbaric nature of Aboriginal society. In 1984 Morgan delivered a rip-roaring speech to the Australian Mining Industry Council reprising all of the above, throwing in the claim that sacred sites were fake, remarking how partial Aborigines were to the "particular flavour" of Chinese flesh, and asking:

> On what grounds can a minister or parliament say, on the one hand we respect, recognise and give legal support to the spiritual claims you have to a very substantial portion of this country, but on the other hand we cannot sanction infanticide, cannibalism and the cruel initiation rites which you regard either as customary or as a matter of religious obligation?

Morgan wasn't perturbed by Asian immigration. Others were. These were the years in which the historian Geoffrey Blainey sought to put a respectable face on dark fears that white Australia was vanishing:

> I do not accept the view, widely held in the Federal Cabinet, that some kind of slow Asian takeover of Australia is inevitable. I do not believe that we are powerless. I do believe that we can with good will and good sense control our destiny ... As a people, we seem to move from extreme to extreme. In the past 30 years the government of Australia has moved from the extreme of wanting a white Australia to the extreme of saying that we will have an Asian Australia and that the quicker we move towards it the better.

Both lines of argument led to the same conclusion: that Australia was turning into a land of tribes; that an inevitable clash of cultures would shatter the nation. Time was running out.

Howard had no quarrel with this argument. But for a quixotic bid by Joh Bjelke-Petersen to become prime minister, Howard may well have won the 1987 election. Rather than distance himself from the Nationals after that catastrophe, he decided to shift into their territory. In the name of "One Australia" he pledged the Coalition to roll back land rights, end affirmative action for Aboriginal Australians, and repudiate multiculturalism, which he called a pessimistic belief "that it is impossible to have an Australian ethos." He had done his arithmetic. The Australian Election Study of voting in the 1987 poll showed 53 per cent of Australians objected to "special benefits" for Indigenous Australians and 57 per cent thought land rights had gone too far. When the politicians moved into their immense new home on the hill in 1988, Hawke proposed the first business of the parliament should be a bipartisan motion recognising prior Aboriginal occupation of Australia. Howard refused.

He also shattered the twenty-year truce on multi-racial immigration. Again, he knew where the votes were. The same AES study showed half the country wanted no more migrants for the moment and half the rest wanted only a small quota for Asians. Howard's move was deliberate, not an off-the-cuff remark on radio. Limiting Asian immigration began as the drafted policy of the Liberal Party, endorsed emphatically by the Nationals. They didn't beat around the bush. "We need," said the Nationals' leader Ian Sinclair, "to reduce the number of Asians." Howard agreed. On radio on 1 August 1988 he called for Asian immigration to be "slowed down a little, so that the capacity of the community to absorb was greater." Howard had done his sums but he had not anticipated the wave of disgust that swept the country as he brought race politics to Canberra. Liberal voters were appalled. The liberal press was brutal. Shadow ministers crossed the floor to repudiate his shift in direction. He became a figure of ridicule, even contempt. Within months, Andrew Peacock was once again leader of the Opposition; Howard would spend the next six years plotting to get his old job back.

The miners, still pouring money into the fight against land rights, stopped Hawke's plans at the border of Western Australia. Then came Mabo in 1992. By this time John Hewson, a retired professor of economics, was leading the Opposition. He saw what Mabo meant and told the Liberal party room this was a moment to rise above politics. Howard accused him of insulting politicians. Beleaguered after his defeat in the "unloseable" election of 1993, Hewson was compelled to fight Keating's native title bill tooth and nail. When some National senators crossed the floor to amend a few of the bill's more obvious shortcomings – and it appeared the Coalition parties might now change tack – Howard rallied the troops to maintain absolute opposition to legislation he declared "rotten to the core." The miners continued their attacks. Again, both politicians and miners claimed the survival of the nation was at stake. Morgan warned audiences up and down the country of the "territorial dismemberment of the Australian continent and the end of the Australian nation as we have known it."

Though Howard had made one or two apologies by the time he clambered back into the saddle in early 1995, he had not remade himself. He was as willing as ever to play the race card in national politics. The lesson he took from his downfall in 1988 was that doing so took great care. He had the skill. Race was to be whispered, not shouted. It was there in the slogan of his 1996 election campaign: "For All of Us." When a bad-tempered candidate in Queensland with no hope of winning her seat voiced out loud many of Howard's own attitudes, he had her sacked. As his biographer, David Barnett, remarked: "Whatever the merits of her opinions, there was no room for her in the campaign."

Hanson was in a unique position. She was on the ballot as a Liberal. The Nationals hadn't bothered to stand a candidate. Her sacking made her a celebrity in Ipswich and news across Australia. No one running for federal office in Oxley had spoken as she did, voicing so directly local contempt for the Aborigines of the town. That it was a woman showing up the men as mealy-mouthed added to the feisty glamour of the candidate. Labor did not contest her race politics head-on. The Liberal machine helped her discreetly behind the scenes. On 2 March 1996, a nearly 20 per cent swing saw her elected the Member for Oxley.

That Hanson appeared in parliament in 1996 with a bunch of men elected essentially by kicking the race can provoked a great deal of soul-searching. There was a sense that the country was tainted by the result. Gerard Henderson, until recently chief of staff to John Howard, wrote:

> There is a shadow over the 1996 Federal election campaign which affects all political parties. Unless removed, its impact will extend well beyond the respective bouts of celebration and teeth-gnashing as political activists wind down after the March 2 poll. Q: What turned Graeme Campbell, Bob Katter and, now, Pauline Hanson into national political figures? A: Proud intolerance – no more, no less.

While Hanson was attacking Aboriginal privilege in Ipswich, Bob Burgess, a National Party man in north Queensland, provoked outrage across the country by remarking that citizenship ceremonies were a "de-wogging exercise." Katter, the party's man in the seat next door, then

denounced his mate's critics as "little slanty-eyed ideologues who perse-
cute ordinary average Australians." Burgess lost on election day but Katter
retained Kennedy with a 22 per cent swing. Meanwhile in Western
Australia, Graeme Campbell, thrown out of the Labor Party for backing
apartheid, campaigning against immigration and addressing the far-right,
anti-Semitic Australian League of Rights, was easily returned in the
immense seat of Kalgoorlie.

What followed was – by today's standards – a frank debate on the role
of race in Australian politics. Neville Bonner, the first Indigenous member of the national parliament and a resident of Oxley, offered grim
resignation. "We know there is a great deal of racism out there because
we come up against it every day of our lives," he said. "There are a lot of
people who quietly applaud racist attitudes without having to declare
themselves. What else can we do but grin and bear it?" Editorials urged
the new prime minister to see the election result as a spur to greater
efforts to combat racism and to resist calls to water down the provisions
of the *Racial Discrimination Act* lately strengthened by the addition of the
anti-hate speech provision 18C. The *Sydney Morning Herald* offered modest
optimism:

> For while it certainly doesn't mean Australia's drive to build a tol-
> erant, multicultural society has failed – remember, the victories
> outlined here were confined to rural or semi-rural Queensland and
> Western Australia – it does stand as a warning that an even bigger
> effort needs to be made to overcome the deep-seated racial preju-
> dice which obviously exists in parts of Australia.

Hanson wasn't having a bar of it. In September she delivered her
maiden speech to a nearly empty House of Representatives, a speech
which turned her from an oddity into a celebrity. It was demotic, blunt
and dripping with contempt for Aborigines and Asians. Andrew Markus
called it "a political masterpiece, one of the most memorable of parliamentary speeches." Hanson was right to boast that she sent "tremors like

an earthquake across the country." But the damage done was not her work alone. Howard refused to contest her. This was the time to take a stand. He didn't. His plan was to wait her out and hope her people would come back to him. But Hanson went from strength to strength. She was stumbling, repetitive and often silly, but somehow rose above the absurdity of her own campaign. And the prime minister was silent.

A NOTE ON THE LANGUAGE

A new political language began to be fashioned in America in the 1980s to combat unwelcome fresh ideas about sex, women, guns, human rights and especially race. The fate of Western civilisation was said to be hanging in the balance. This lingo of reaction was hammered out in Washington think-tanks and test-run in little magazines. Big minds and big money were engaged in the task. The work was wonderfully done. A key purpose of the exercise was to find ways in a disapproving world of continuing to fight for white privilege. Talk of *culture wars*, *elites* and *political correctness* offered cover to politicians as they went about an old familiar task.

Australia lapped it up. An early adopter was the mining industry. The industry's mouthpiece, the Institute of Public Affairs, became quickly fluent in the newspeak. So did News Limited, which was the bridge on which this American dialect crossed into Australian public life. Decades later, hardly a week − hardly a day − goes by without an opinion piece in the *Australian* deploring *political correctness* and/or the blindness of the *elites*. The language would not have stuck without there being, often enough, a grain of truth in the writing of the harpy columnists. Yes, there are *progressives* who don't give a damn about the people they claim to speak for. And there are *politically correct* politicians afraid of being branded bigots or traitors if they show their true colours. Such horrors have been with us always and the English language has always had ways of dealing with them. The point of the new rhetoric isn't so much argument as abuse. Yet it comes with an attractive plea that we debate race and sex and guns and free speech without abusing one another. "You ought to be able to have sensible discussion on these sorts of things," John Howard told Paul Kelly and Dennis Shanahan last year. "But there is a sense in which people are so frightened of being accused of being discriminatory or intolerant that they don't speak the commonsense view."

Evidence of speech silenced is scant. In late February, on the seventh straight day attacking *Q&A* panellist Yassmin Abdel-Magied, the *Australian* published a cartoon by Bill Leak which, not so long ago, would have been considered unthinkable in a national newspaper. Leak has a hipster teacher telling primary-school children: "Out of cultural sensitivity to the beliefs of some of our more devout Muslim pupils we have decided to relax the school rule banning the beheading of infidels." Meanwhile, on the opposite page, Janet Albrechtsen was for the umpteenth time denouncing the anti-insult, anti-intimidation provision of the *Racial Discrimination Act* as "a law that strikes at the heart of Western liberalism." How? Who is it silencing at the *Oz*? Could Bill Leak's abuse have been any more robust? Yet Albrechtsen worked herself up into a fury over the Turnbull government's failure to free Australia from the act:

> It's time to change the party's name to the Illiberal Party. And in that values vacuum you will hear Pauline Hanson's tally-counter clicking fast and furiously as more voters choose One Nation rather than a misleadingly labelled Liberal government that cannot find the political backbone to defend free speech.

Speakers of newspeak have many enemies in their sights. Some are virtual strangers on the Australian political scene. It mattered in America to fashion a vivid new language to attack anyone who might aid abortion or regulate gun ownership. They aren't such urgent causes here, though it's a pleasure to hear One Nation's Malcolm Roberts slip into the lingo to denounce those wishing to punish gun smugglers as "enemies of freedom." Done by the book. But the common enemies are many, and here and abroad two underlying principles are always in play when new rhetoric is deployed: the Left is the enemy of freedom, and race is never about race. Some key terms:

Assimilation: "Asians," warned Hanson in her maiden speech, "have their own culture and religion, form ghettos and do not assimilate." Not being able to fit in to a new country is a key racist claim through the ages. Once blood and biology were to blame. That's become unfashionable. Now the fault is said to lie with culture and religion. Asians were bad enough but

Muslims are worse. On her return to parliament in 2016 she declared: "Now we are in danger of being swamped by Muslims, who bear a culture and ideology that is incompatible with our own."

Cosmopolitan: Men and women of the world and their shallow ideas. Not really Australian. Backers of *multiculturalism* are by definition *cosmopolitan*. Ditto, rich republicans like Malcolm Turnbull. Out on the far right, *cosmopolitans* are blamed for seeking to impose a police state in order to ban guns.

Culture war: The notion that new ideas on race, sex, religion, freedom, education and so on are a coordinated attack on Western values that must be met with full force on all fronts. The metaphor of war signals the threat and conscripts contestants into two armies – Attackers and Defenders – while licensing ferocious combat in the trenches. John Howard was the Monash of culture warriors, but these days only his old army seems to be in the field. The other got bored and left.

Division: The natural consequence of pampering Aborigines or allowing foreigners into the country who won't assimilate. "This nation is being divided into black and white," Hanson declared in 1996. "I am fed up with being told, 'This is our land.' Well, where the hell do I go?" The threat of Aboriginal partition seems to have receded in Hanson's mind, while the danger of *multiculturalism* is as potent as ever. She has always said: "Abolishing the policy of multiculturalism will save billions of dollars and allow those from ethnic backgrounds to join mainstream Australia, paving the way to a strong, united country." Hence the party name: One Nation.

Elites: Not men who lunch at the Melbourne Club. Not families who find themselves in the *BRW* Rich List. But educated and prosperous Australians who live in cities and impose their *progressive* ideas on the *mainstream*. Hanson declared on the day of Trump's victory: "People around the world are saying, 'We've had enough with the major political parties, with the establishment, with the elites.'" Their influence is sinister. They bully. They seize control of universities. The ABC is staffed with *elites*. Hanson's 1997 manifesto used language familiar from attacks on Jews before World War II: "Our common oppressors are a class of raceless, placeless, cosmopolitan elites who are exercising almost absolute power over us: like black spiders above the wheels of industry, they are spinning the webs of our destiny."

Equality: "My greatest desire is to see all Australians treat each other as equals," says Hanson. Another key racist concept: that need and not race should decide who gets what. Sometimes expressed: "I am colour-blind." Fine in theory. But in Hanson's world it means cheap loans for farmers but no scholarships for black kids. She electrified the nation in her maiden speech by declaring: "I am fed up to the back teeth with the inequalities that are being promoted by the government and paid for by the taxpayer under the assumption that Aboriginals are the most disadvantaged people in Australia."

Free speech: Not about everything. Mainly race. But it's not free speech to ping racists for being racists. That's censorship or, indeed, persecution. Not at issue here is Australia's status as the only country in the Western world without a Bill of Rights. The battleground is section 18C of the *Racial Discrimination Act*, which seeks to put a brake – no fines, no jail time – on speech that might "offend, insult, humiliate or intimidate" people on the basis of their "race, colour or national or ethnic origin." A complex debate continues between those who want the law to stay as it is (nearly everyone); reformists who want to raise the bar by deleting offend and insult; and abolitionists who claim that being able to humiliate and intimidate Jews and Lebanese is essential to free speech. By driving this debate, News Limited has made 18C the most famous single provision in Australian law.

Mainstream: Not to be confused with majority. Numbers don't count. The mainstream is white, of Christian background and conservative. Commonsense and true Australian values, in such short supply among the *elites*, flourish in the mainstream. *Assimilation* means merging with the mainstream. Care must be taken not to call overwhelmingly popular causes like equal marriage *mainstream*. The word doesn't work like that. Also: while *mainstream* is obviously good, the *mainstream media* is self-evidently bad.

Multiculturalism: The policy of allowing many cultures to survive – or even flourish – in a single country. From the moment she emerged from Marsden's Seafoods, Hanson's primary target has been *multiculturalism*. Over the last twenty years she's found a good word to say from time to time about Muslims and Aboriginals, but not *multiculturalism*. She is the voice of that 12 per cent of Australians who, according to the latest Scanlon survey, disagree that *multiculturalism* has been good for Australia. On her return to parliament in 2016 she declared: "Indiscriminate immigration and aggressive multiculturalism have caused crime to escalate and trust and social cohesion to decline. Too many Australians are afraid to walk alone at night in their neighbourhoods. Too many of us live in fear of terrorism."

Politically correct or *PC*: A protean term for which new uses are found every day. *PC* began life when American communists in the 1930s criticised the rigid doctrines of Joseph Stalin as "politically correct." Something of that meaning remains after all these years: *PC* is sticking with beliefs that are doctrinaire and out of touch with reality. Hanson has dismissed just about everything she disagrees with as *PC*: special treatment for Aborigines; tenderness to refugees; *multiculturalism* in all its forms; indulging the unemployed; any and all "unworkable socialist engineering doctrines"; and lately a satirical Meat & Livestock Australia advertisement which had a dozen races gathering for a beach barbeque on Australia Day. "Surely you have all had enough of politically correct stupidity like this," raged Hanson. "It has to stop because it is undermining our Australian culture."

PC also has another meaning: cowardice in debate or ridiculous lengths taken to prevent giving offence. The Urban Dictionary: "Only pathetically weak people that don't have the balls to say what they feel and mean are politically correct pussies." The fundamental charge of harpy columnists is: "He doesn't believe what he's saying about blacks/women/refugees/

homosexuals/Muslims, he is just being *politically correct*." Cowardice is shackling debate. Oddly, there seems no requirement that the cowardice be proved. It just is.

Populism: The front-bar wisdom that sees the world divided between them and us, where the good are always oppressed by the self-serving few. Those on the left blame the rich. Those on the right, the elites.

Progressive: Pejorative. Useful synonym for both *left* and *elite*. Progressives sit on both sides of politics. They have no real feeling for the men and women whose interests they claim to have at heart. Progressives are even to blame for the rise of Donald Trump. Wayne Swan sees it as a lesson for Australia: "If you're looking for reasons for Trump's victory look no further than the potent combination of powerful vested interests dictating policy and some progressive elites shoving their orthodoxies down working people's throats."

Swamped: Not a fact but a state of mind. We're waiting for the new census figures, but the last showed Asians at 8 per cent of the population. Muslims numbers are growing but the Australian Bureau of Statistics has them at the moment at only a little over 2 per cent of the population.

Western Civilisation: Old and fragile, Christian and white. Its oldest continuing institutions are, according to Tony Abbott, the papacy and the crown. Western Civilisation is under continuous attack today from progressive ideas and the long collapse of public morals. Australia has earned a fine reputation in the conservative world as a last redoubt in the struggle to defend Western Civilisation, for example by resisting equal marriage. Supercharging Australia's efforts will be the $25-million Ramsay Centre for Western Civilisation, to be chaired by John Howard. Abbott is on the board. An early task may be to clarify where the Australian Way of Life stands vis-à-vis Western Civilisation. This is not entirely clear. The old enemy of Western Civilisation is, of course, Occidental Civilisation.

"If there is a little bit of grease still on me, not washed off from the fish shop, you'll understand," Hanson said with a girlish laugh. But even from the back row of Ulverstone's Leven Theatre you could see there wasn't so much as a speck of lint on that perfectly ironed jungle-green jersey suit. It was May 1997 and I was trailing Hanson around Tasmania, as keen to watch her crowds as her. Looking back it's clear this was almost the last hurrah of politics by public meeting. She was a trouper with an old-fashioned story building a following town by town, demonstration by demonstration. In Hobart, Launceston and now up on the "Paradise Coast" of Tasmania the pattern was the same: a candlelit vigil in the streets that would turn rowdy before the night was out, and a full house ready to give Hanson ovation after ovation as she delivered her mean message of self-help and equality.

Ulverstone was billed in those days as an epicentre of suicide, unemployment and dashed dreams. But Hanson's crowd was doing okay. Women in the vigil told me: (a) men found her sexy because she was a working woman who looked after herself, and (b) though maybe her followers weren't doing as well as they once did, they were doing fine. They weren't on their uppers. And they weren't planning to share their modest prosperity with blacks, Asians or the world. To her purse-proud audiences in Tasmania she held out the prospect of saving money by cutting every government program designed to help Aborigines, foreigners, immigrants and single mothers. Race was the chilli in the mix. She won ovations every time she brought money and race together. When she listed the suburbs where "we" feel like foreigners in our own land – all on the mainland: Cabramatta, Surfers Paradise, Richmond, etc. – her people gave her all their attention. When she pledged to get the UN off Australia's back, the applause raised the roof.

Hanson was riding high. She had sold the shop and set up her own party. But from the start there was this problem: it was only ever about her. The name of the party said everything: "Pauline Hanson's One Nation." She had complaints rather than policies. There were crowds but no movement. Without her, One Nation wouldn't last a week. But she needed collaborators. Ultimately, her fate depended on the men and women of the little court she gathered around her. She did not pick well. Out on the political fringe there are always strange characters on the loose eager to attach themselves – and their causes – to power. Bush anti-Semites were piling into her Queensland branches. Gun fanatics were signing up to One Nation, spruiking their claim that Port Arthur never happened. Her host on this whistlestop tour of Tasmania – and head of the new state branch of One Nation – was Chester Somerville, a chocolate seller from Hobart who was once president of the Tasmanian National Party before founding the Concerned Voters Association dedicated to keeping sodomy a crime on the island.

Hanson had already shed her first Svengali. John Pasquarelli appeared within a few days of her election win. The former crocodile hunter was a creature of the far right, having worked for the renegade MP for Kalgoorlie, Graeme Campbell. He and Hanson saw eye to eye on Aborigines. Hanson explained: "John wanted a job, and Graeme needed someone to second his motions." Pasquarelli lasted eight months. He taught her the ropes. He vetted her interviews and wrote her early speeches. She says she found the courage to reject his draft of her maiden speech after he took her to hear the ancient Bob Santamaria celebrating some big anniversary of the Catholic far right. What a small world: Santa helped Pauline find her voice.

David Oldfield turned up the night of the maiden speech. He persuaded her to sack Pasquarelli. They had an affair. "I came to learn he spent more time in the bathroom than any woman I know, including me." Oldfield was a failed Liberal candidate with aggressive views on Aborigines and migrants, who had a job in Tony Abbott's office. Abbott would later say: "Even Jesus had his Judas." Oldfield and a professional fundraiser called David Ettridge set up One Nation with a structure designed to protect the party from infiltration. While Hanson was castigating politicians for not listening to the people, she was putting together a party that never had to listen to its followers. There were only ever three members: Oldfield, Ettridge and her. On a night of protests and smashed windows it was launched in Ipswich in April 1997.

These were great months for Voltaire. His name was often on Hanson's lips as she battled her way round Tasmania. Howard cited the philosopher's passion for liberty as he resolutely ignored all pleas to engage with Hanson. He labelled her parliamentary debut a triumph of free speech:

> One of the great changes that has come over Australia in the last six months is that people do feel able to speak a little more freely and a little more openly about what they feel. In a sense the pall of censorship on certain issues has been lifted ... I think there has been a change and I think that's a very good thing.

Even when he ventured to correct her and once or twice even question the balance of her mind, he never called her a racist. He was at pains to defend her followers:

> Pauline Hanson was something of a metaphor for a group of Australians, most of whom did not have a racist bone in their bodies, who believed that in different ways they had been passed over ...

Within weeks of the party's launch, Newspoll had One Nation at 7 per cent of the national vote. While there was some confusion among commentators about where her support was coming from, Howard knew she presented little danger to Labor. Her people were from the heartland of the National Party. He wrote in his memoir *Lazarus Rising*:

> Could the impact of Hanson have been less if I had attacked her more strongly and openly immediately after her maiden speech? I think not. Pauline Hanson was an accident, but accidents constantly happen in politics. A more vigorous response from me would have intensified the frustrations felt by those Australians to whom she

gave a voice, and gratuitously alienated them from me – and for what purpose, other than the political benefit of the ALP?

Something grubby entered national life at this point. Once again, when it really mattered, Howard showed himself unable to rise above politics. Instead of taking her on in the name of decent Australia, he put the race vote in play in Canberra. What mattered for him was the arithmetic: winning back those lost votes at the fringe. He believed she would soon fizzle out – and all the sooner if the ABC and Fairfax would stop paying her so much attention: "To my mind, the Australian media, with a few notable exceptions such as the Sydney radio talkback host Alan Jones, completely overreacted to Pauline Hanson."

Meanwhile, he would keep his mouth shut and nudge the Coalition into One Nation territory. He slashed funding to Indigenous people, cut immigration numbers, tightly restricted family reunion visas, cut welfare for migrants, tried his best to neuter native title and closed Australia to boat people. Hanson had called for each of these policies. "Howard was smart," she boasted. "He gauged the support I had from the public and, when the time was right, implemented them as Liberal policy."

Hanson survived her own absurdity to triumph at the 1998 Queensland elections. By this time, Channel 7 had broadcast her message from the grave: "Fellow Australians. If you are seeing me now, it means I have been murdered ..." This was meat and drink for Simon Hunt as Pauline Pantsdown and his brilliant compilations of Hansonisms. She sued to prevent the ABC broadcasting "I'm a Backdoor Man" (this was no time for Voltaire) and Hunt retaliated with "I Don't Like It", which proved an even bigger hit:

> I don't like it, no, no, no I don't, never did,
> I don't like it, I don't like anything!
> I don't like it, no, no, no I don't nowhere near
> I don't like it, I don't like anything!

Hanson also published *The Truth*, a collection of speeches and essays that took the One Nation agenda to the edge of farce. She put her name to a dystopian vision of Australia in 2050 absorbed into a United States of Asia under the leadership of Poona Li Hung, a lesbian of mixed race who was somehow or other part human and part machine.

Yet Hanson was still mobbed in bush towns across Queensland and Howard continued to insist the Coalition preference One Nation in the looming state poll. This appalled many Liberals. Howard's deputy, Peter Costello, the premier of Victoria, Jeff Kennett, the NSW leader of the Opposition, Peter Collins, and Malcolm Fraser all wanted to put as much distance as possible between their party and Hanson. They publicly urged Howard to preference One Nation last. He refused. He was counting the numbers and saw that the only hope of saving the failing government of Rob Borbidge was to appease One Nation.

The strategy proved a disaster. From the moment the deal was known, disgusted Liberals began to walk. Eugene White, a lawyer and former party branch president, resigned in writing:

> The Liberal Party generally and the Queensland division in particu-
> lar have displayed total cynicism, abject cowardice, latent racism and
> a complete lack of principle in failing to rule out any preference deal
> with the One Nation party ... John Howard's easy rhetoric hides a
> wily politician who has taken this party and the Government to dark
> places where I do not wish to go, and will go no further.

Paul Kelly wrote in *The March of the Patriots* that the deal with Hanson cost the Liberals nearly a third of its Brisbane vote. And Hanson couldn't enforce her end of the deal. Her voters aren't tractable. They pride themselves on their independence. They make up their own minds. In any case, few of them received how-to-vote cards, because Hanson didn't have the troops to man many booths. So on polling day, the advantage was hers. She won 22 per cent of the primary vote, which with Coalition preferences delivered her eleven seats — five from the Nationals and six from Labor. Labor picked up enough seats with the help of angry Liberals to bring down Borbidge. No insurgent party had ever made such a spectacular debut in Australia. Kelly drew the conclusion that "in two-party-preferred terms Hanson was a vote transfer machine from the Coalition to Labor."

Howard at last got the point. The arithmetic spoke for itself. The 1998 federal poll, only months away, was going to be close. A deal with Hanson would likely deliver power to Labor. It was also clear to the prime minister that he would never be able to persuade the state branches of the party, particularly Victoria, to do a deal with Hanson. If Liberals walked away from the party in Brisbane, think what they would do in Sydney and Melbourne. So after the Queensland catastrophe a decision was taken by the Liberals that would hold – with only occasional slippage – for twenty years: Hanson would go last on the ticket. At least on polling day, her party would be treated as a pariah. That became a fundamental political understanding in this country until another conservative state government way past its prime gambled on Hanson to save the day ...

After Queensland, pundits spoke of One Nation winning half a dozen seats in the Senate. Hanson's own position was more difficult. Fate had once again cursed her with a redistribution and she was fighting an uphill battle in Blair, a new seat carved out of Oxley. Her national campaign faltered. Hate and fear were always her strengths but she was now being quizzed about the eccentric policies One Nation had imported along with so many of its candidates from the far right. She wasn't making headlines anymore. Crowds were smaller and demonstrators had almost disappeared. Television footage was banal. Tension between her and Oldfield was palpable. He was standing for the Senate and spent hours – literally hours – filming himself at country shows in the hope of a few moments on television. In his own mind he had already decided he would leave this "little redhead from Ipswich" behind. One wet morning on the campaign trail, two or three journalists came to Hanson's rescue. She was due at the Henty Show on a day of ankle-deep mud. All she had were open-toe shoes. We found her some boots in Albury. On my hands and knees in front of her, I said: "Of all the things I ever imagined might happen in my life as a journalist, I never thought I'd be fitting Pauline Hanson with gumboots." She smiled in a friendly way and said something that sounded like the call of a seabird: "Earaahecht."

One Nation was all but wiped out. She won a million Senate votes across the nation and the highest vote in Blair but the deals done saw her seat go to the Liberals and only a single One Nation senator elected in Queensland. Both Labor and the Coalition preferenced against her. It was bravely done. "The major parties were willing to take a few hits – Labor electing Liberals, and vice versa – in order to keep One Nation out," explained Antony Green, the ABC's psephologist. By his count, three of Hanson's Senate candidates were blocked this way. All were blocked in the lower house. She vented her disbelief:

> In the House of Representatives, One Nation polled 8.43 per cent of the vote and the National Party 5.29 per cent and they won sixteen seats and One Nation none. This does not reflect the wishes of the Australian voters.

She had a point. But the strategies pioneered at the 1998 poll would keep her out of the Senate, the Legislative Council of New South Wales and the Queensland parliament for nearly twenty years – often by only a few hundred votes.

She retreated to her house on the hill outside Ipswich, but her constituency remained and appeasing them continued to be a priority for Howard. Ironically, she was no longer in Canberra when she had the greatest impact on the country. The boats were back – not many, but an upsurge in numbers. So Howard took an idea Hanson had floated in the 1998 election: that refugees be given only temporary entry. He refined it: boat people would only be allowed into Australia on probation. Welfare benefits would be meagre. Their families would not be allowed to join them. This new regime didn't deter boat people. The boats continued to come.

But now lone adults could no longer cross to make a beachhead for their families. From late 1999, when Labor's Kim Beazley joined forces with Howard to create this new, punitive visa, the smugglers' boats began filling with women and children.

One Nation had fallen to pieces in Queensland. All Hanson's MPs had quit after she and her lieutenants refused to give them a say in the running of the party. Hanson also sacked a number of her close lieutenants. Others walked. Her old friend Heather Hill left complaining about the head office in Manly refusing to account for the spending of nearly $5 million. "I don't have the foggiest where it has gone." Ettridge resigned in January 2000. Later that year Hanson sacked Oldfield, who was setting up a little political empire of his own from a perch in the NSW Legislative Council. But even in all this chaos One Nation was able to win three seats in the West Australian upper house in February 2001 and help install the Labor government of Geoff Gallop. A week later, fresh elections were held in Queensland. Most of her old troops were swept from parliament but One Nation's preferences delivered Peter Beattie Labor's biggest victory in the state for over sixty years. Hanson was doing no deals. Her voters were left to decide for themselves which party would have their preferences. By this time the pattern was clear. Instead of returning whence they came – mainly the Nationals – they split roughly 50/50. About half returned to the Coalition, but the other half crossed to Labor. This is what made One Nation so dangerous even when its primary vote was small: it bled votes to Labor. John Howard, who faced his own election sometime before Christmas, found his fortunes had sunk very low.

Hanson had campaigned fiercely in both state polls against the refugees now arriving by boat in even greater numbers. Her solution was simple: a blockade. "We go out, we meet them, we fill them up with fuel, fill them up with food, give them medical supplies and we say, 'Go that way.' " The blockade began the day the navy shipped off to a prison camp on Nauru the 433 refugees rescued by the *Tampa*. Australia had started down a path from which there appears to be no return. A week later, the

World Trade Center was brought down by al-Qaeda. The two narratives had nothing to do with one another but Howard wove them together superbly. He wrapped race in the flag. Again, he took his cue from Hanson. In her maiden speech she had said: "If I can invite whom I want into my home, then I should have the right to have a say in who comes into my country." Howard put it rather better at the launch of the Liberal Party's 2001 campaign in Sydney's City Recital Hall:

> National security is … about a proper response to terrorism. It's also about having a far-sighted, strong, well-thought-out defence policy. It is also about having an uncompromising view about the fundamental right of this country to protect its borders. It's about this nation saying to the world we are a generous, open-hearted people taking more refugees on a per capita basis than any nation except Canada, we have a proud record of welcoming people from 140 different nations. But we will decide who comes to this country and the circumstances in which they come.

This was the campaign slogan. We all knew it. From the balcony of this elegant recital hall I watched the crowd of Liberals go wild. These prosperous white Australians were baying for border protection. The ranks of candidates were on their feet. They sensed victory. Survivors of the old Liberal left who once sacked Howard for playing the race card gave him a standing ovation. Philip Ruddock was one of their number in 1988, but now as Minister for Immigration he was modestly acknowledging the applause pouring down on his head. Politics in Australia had shifted.

Howard had made Hanson redundant. Her party was a shot duck. She had already been charged with electoral fraud. Even so, she nearly won a Senate seat in the *Tampa* election. Her vote – 10 per cent – was a little better than her party had won in 1998. But this time it didn't deliver a senator. She needed a few preferences. They didn't come. The same parties that filched her policies in the campaign organised against her at the poll. The irony is easily lost. Tim Colebatch wrote recently on *Inside Story*: "In those days, her simple ignorant racism, so typical of the Australia she grew up in, was seen as beyond the pale." Not really. It had entered the political mix of the nation. After days of counting, tubby Ron Boswell of the Nationals beat Hanson for the last Senate spot in Queensland. He would look back on this as the greatest achievement of his career. She was written off everywhere. But her constituency remained. This was not the end of the show, only the interval.

Australia came late to the game. Since 1948, Americans have been polled after each election to find out why they voted as they did. The Swedes started to take these national snapshots in the 1950s and the British in the 1960s. Belfast-born Ian McAllister began the Australian Election Study after Bob Hawke's third victory in 1987. From his post at the ANU – where these days he is Distinguished Professor of Political Science – McAllister has conducted a dozen of these big, after-the-event surveys over thirty years. "We ask how people made their choices: the effect of the election campaign, the effect of the longer-term predisposi- tions, the background characteristics, the political socialisation. It's about trying to unravel all of these various things that come together to make simply a choice on a ballot paper."

McAllister's questions are controversial. The political science industry feeds off the Australian Election Studies. Dinner parties break up in con- fusion as pollsters and academics bicker over questions asked and not asked. McAllister told me: "If I put in every question that everybody emailed me or wrote to me about, you'd have a thousand-page question- naire and nobody would fill it in." He says the point of the surveys sent to thousands of voters after each poll is continuity. "When you've got exactly the same question being asked consistently over a period of time using essentially the same methodology, you've got an unusually reliable measure of something."

The Australian voter is a species he has come to admire deeply. "First of all they have to go to the polls more than any other voter in the world that I can possibly imagine. And secondly they have to deal with a range of com- plexity in electoral systems, in terms of casting a vote, which again defies anything in any other society. So the Australian voter, I think, is pretty over- burdened by politics." Yet they remain thoughtful. "People don't make whimsical choices by and large. They do look at policies." They are not volatile. "We found in our surveys early in the piece about 70 per cent of people never ever change their vote from the very first election they voted in to the last election before they died. These days it's around about 50 per cent. So basically most people don't change. And when people do change it's a relatively small proportion that change from election to election."

That we've been so stable makes McAllister particularly alert to "the unexpected long-term decline" of trust in the political class, in career politicians, in democracy itself. "Australia has stood apart from a lot of other countries because it's had very high levels of satisfaction with democracy historically, some of the highest in the world, second only to one or two Scandinavian countries." He dates the slide from 2010. Elections since haven't provided the usual upswings of faith and hope. The numbers have kept falling. "One of the things I observe in our surveys is the proportion of people that believe the government would have a positive effect on the economy in the future year was at its lowest level we've ever recorded in 2016. So people don't have confidence in the government ... They see this quick turnover in leaders. They see scandals to do with expenses, and so on. And they become very jaded. And then I think we've had a lack of decisive leadership as well. I mean Rudd Mark I was the last popular leader that existed in Australia. We haven't had one since."

Ever since McAllister gathered the first set of One Nation numbers in 1998, political scientists have been disputing what they mean. Do they show people flocking to Hanson because of the flags she flies – particularly on race – or are they falling in with her simply because they're disenchanted with the political system? McAllister sees a shift from one to the other: "My sense this time is that ONP#2 doesn't really stand for much, other than being anti-establishment, whereas ONP#1 had a more definable policy basis. So Pauline Hanson is tapping into the prevailing political distrust in career politicians from both sides." But others citing the same material come to the opposite conclusion. More of this dispute later. It's fundamental to understanding the challenge Hanson poses to public life in this country. Is she a party of policy or protest? Hanson is a puzzle with consequences.

McAllister ran the One Nation numbers from the latest AES for this Quarterly Essay. They are the best available evidence of who Hanson's voters were and what they wanted at the 2016 elections. The numbers come with a caveat from McAllister: "Treat the survey data — because of the small numbers of ONP supporters — as a blurry image rather than a precise profile." Even so, as we picked our way through the material together, McAllister identified issues where One Nation's views emerge in full focus. Andrew Markus also commented on the figures for me, as did Murray Goot of Macquarie University, an expert on polling with a particular interest in the One Nation vote who has often taken a contrary view to McAllister. Finally, I've drawn into the discussion several professional pollsters who have conducted focus groups among resurgent One Nation voters since the elections in the bush, in towns and, these days more than ever, in capital cities.

National background

One Nation voters in 2016 were almost entirely native-born Australians. Not even newcomers from the UK or New Zealand were drawn to Hanson's party. Her people are absolutely ours and One Nation is the most Aussie party of them all.

Liberal	78 per cent native-born
Labor	79 per cent
Greens	82 per cent
National	91 per cent
One Nation	98 per cent

Age and sex

One Nation is a party of old people but there's no sign they are dying out. According to the AES figures, roughly a third of Hanson's voters in 2016 were under the age of forty-four. And women are voting One Nation. Back in the 1990s, voters were mostly men. That's shifted. Here's the split:

	1998	2016
Male	65	56
Female	35	44

Reports from focus groups suggest these are working women, better educated than the men. "They looked like nice Labor voters working in nice jobs," said one researcher. "We had a childcare worker, two government workers, and I think there was a teacher. Yet they like Pauline." Other reports from focus groups suggest contradictions here: "Women like her because she's a woman who speaks her mind. Men like her because she's a woman who stands up against feminism." That she's a woman from the "life doesn't owe us anything" school is a key aspect of her political make-up. Raising four children from two husbands hasn't softened her heart towards single mothers. Twice divorced, she backs men burnt by the divorce courts. She opposes extending paid parental leave by two weeks: "They get themselves pregnant and have the same problems did with the Baby Bonus, with people just doing it for the money."

Class

Most One Nation voters see themselves as working class. McAllister calls that "pretty clear." This hasn't changed in twenty years. Hanson's people may have aspirations but they don't see themselves coming up in the world.

Greens	24 per cent identify as working class
Liberal	32 per cent
Labor	45 per cent
National	46 per cent
One Nation	66 per cent

Religion

Hanson is not pulling the religious vote. Rebecca Huntley, social researcher and former director of Ipsos Australia, says: "We're a little shielded from the worst implications of the rise of the Trump vote by the fact that this is not a highly religious group." Hanson's staunch defence of Christianity in the face of Muslim hordes isn't about faith but preserving our way of life. Hanson's moral agenda is to punish welfare bludgers not perverts. One Nation voters rarely worship. While 48 per cent of Australians never attend church – not even for weddings and funerals – the figure for One Nation voters is 60 per cent. Breakaway Cory Bernardi is pursuing a tiny constituency that believes in small government and high Catholic morality. Hanson backs neither: she's a secular, big government woman. That's a big constituency.

Where do they live?

Both the city and the bush. One Nation has always had a strong city presence despite its image as a bush party. Labor Party research and focus groups report strong growth of support for One Nation in seats on the fringe of big towns and capital cities, seats on the edge of – but not actually among – migrant suburbs. This appears to be a pattern across Australia. On the edge of Sydney in 2016, One Nation picked up over 6 per cent of the Senate vote in Lindsay (75 per cent Australian-born) but only 3 per cent a few kilometres away in Greenway (58 per cent Australian-born). In Lindsay they have fears rather than experience. As one researcher told me: "When you probe for personal experiences on anything they say about welfare or immigration, it's always second- and third-hand."

	One Nation 1998	One Nation 2016	General public 2016
Rural/village	18	17	10
Small towns	17	10	11
Bigger towns	27	29	23
Cities	39	44	57

Reports from focus groups suggest city folk most respect Hanson. "The bush is more sceptical of One Nation than the cities," says one researcher. "In the bush they tend to say she doesn't have the answers. Those in the cities are more in agreement with her. They rate her intelligence in the city. They say she's doing better, she's learnt a lot. In the country they think she's a bit stupid."

How educated are they?

Then and now, the figures show the typical One Nation voter didn't finish school. Yet they are not unqualified. They make an effort. Tradespeople are strongly represented in party ranks. But eight out of ten have never set foot on a university campus. "That's the big political effect," says McAllister.

	2016	
	One Nation	General public
Diploma	12	9
Non-trade qualification	15	9
Trade	30	15
University	20	42
No qualification	21	25

Education is the clearest link between Hanson, Trump and Brexit. Surveys here, in the United States and in the United Kingdom all point to education as a key component of political dissatisfaction. In the UK, Matthew Goodwin and Oliver Heath found "educational inequality" was the strongest driver of Brexit. In the US, Nate Silver concluded, "the education gap is carving up the American electorate and toppling political coalitions that had been in place for many years."

That about eight out of ten One Nation voters dropped out of school doesn't mark them as dumb. Queensland, the party's heartland, made it extraordinarily hard for a long time for poor kids to get to university. But for whatever reason, few of Hanson's people have been exposed to life and learning on a campus. Huntley wonders if "the persistent attachment to clearly illogical connections between, say, asylum seekers and crime waves, and also the interest in non-official online content, is because they

never had at least some exposure to what happens at higher education."
What strikes her in focus groups is the One Nation attitude: "I can work
this all out by myself."

Have they been ruined by globalisation?

No. They are in work and middling prosperous. They aren't on welfare.
McAllister's figures suggest there's nothing particularly special about the
pattern of employment for Hanson's people. One Nation voters are no
more likely to be at the bottom of the management heap than anyone else.
There's a tiny – and perhaps unreliable – skew away from government
employment. McAllister says, "That's a reflection of the fact that they tend
not to have higher education."

But Hanson's people are oddly gloomy about their prospects. One of
the questions always asked in the AES is: "How does the financial situation of your own household compare with what it was twelve months
ago?" This is the breakdown by party of those who thought things were
now "a little" or "a lot" worse for them than a year ago:

National	25 per cent
Green	27 per cent
Liberal	29 per cent
Labor	38 per cent
One Nation	68 per cent

The same gloom is apparent when Hanson's people are asked about the
state of the economy. This is the breakdown of those who thought the
national economy was "a little" or "a lot" worse than it was a year ago:

National	35 per cent
Green	44 per cent
Labor	46 per cent
Liberal	47 per cent
One Nation	73 per cent

So while there is a lot of gloom about, Hanson's people see the national economy going to hell in a handcart. Why?

The standard explanation – that these are people left behind by globalisation – works for Trump's voters and is strong in the mix with Brexit. But it seems not a decisive component of the Hanson vote. This country weathered the GFC in good shape. There is not a ruined class that lost their houses and savings in the crash. Employment held up. Economic growth since has been better in the cities – where half Hanson's voters live – than the country, but her people are in work. Focus groups say many One Nation voters are working part-time when they would like to be full-time. Many worry about losing their jobs because they fear a new job will be hard to find. But sheeting those fears home to the ravages of free trade is difficult. Queensland is a free-trade state. Key to every trade deal this nation has signed in the last few decades is attempting to open world markets to coal, cattle and sugar. Nor does general nervousness about employment distinguish these voters from very many Australians. If Hanson were the natural choice of those wishing they had a better job and fearful of losing the one they have, she should be commanding divisions, not battalions.

The exaggerated gloom of One Nation voters in the 2016 election goes to something deeper than the economy. One Nation is the nostalgia party. "Simply addressing economic inequality – which is what the left has tried to do – is just not sufficient," says Huntley. "Prosperity is important, but what worries this group is the cultural, social slippage they feel in their life. They imagine their fathers' and grandfathers' lives were better, more certain, easier to navigate. Maybe they were and maybe they weren't, but it's the loss of that that is worrying for them. The economic argument alone isn't persuasive for them."

But of course it has to be addressed. "If they think that a political party is representing their economic interest, they will vote for that party," says Kosmos Samaras, assistant state secretary of the Labor Party in Victoria. "But if the party doesn't, they'll vote on other interests."

By that he means alienation and hostility to immigration. "They feel: 'I'm getting screwed anyway, so I'm just going to turn up to vote and fuck them.'"

Immigration

The numbers are powerful. Twenty years ago Hanson's people were hostile to immigration. Now they are extraordinarily so. One Nation is the party of those not bought off in the end by Howard's great Faustian pact: close the borders to boat people and the nation will relax about mass immigration.

Over 80 per cent of One Nation voters considered immigration "extremely important" when deciding how to vote. It's a number that puts Hanson's party way outside the pack:

Green	40 per cent
Labor	43 per cent
Liberal	49 per cent
National	54 per cent
One Nation	82 per cent

Over 80 per cent of One Nation voters also want immigration numbers cut. The wishes of the party are now even more extreme than they were twenty years ago. In 2016 the AES turned up only a single One Nation voter happy to see immigration increased. The numbers went all the other way. This puts Hanson's people dramatically at odds with the sentiment of a welcoming country. Those in each party calling for immigration numbers to be cut "a lot":

Green	7 per cent
Labor	21 per cent
Liberal	24 per cent
National	32 per cent
One Nation	83 per cent

Their grim attitudes to migrants also set Hanson's people apart. For One Nation voters, there is little disagreement that migrants increase crime, are not good for the economy and take the jobs of native-born Australians. Those in each party who "agree" or "strongly agree" that migrants:

	Increase crime:	Are good for the economy:	Take our jobs:
Green	10	83	11
Labor	35	60	31
Liberal	42	50	30
Nationals	47	40	36
One Nation	79	10	67

For most Australian voters the boats are a problem solved. Not for the Greens. They are appalled by Manus and Nauru and alone continue to oppose the policy of naval blockade and turning back the boats. What sets One Nation apart here is the near-unanimous support in party ranks for that strategy. It stands to reason: this unique policy began as a Hanson special. Those in each party who "agree" or "strongly agree" with turnbacks:

Green	10 per cent
Labor	55 per cent
Liberal	63 per cent
National	63 per cent
One Nation	90 per cent

One Nation is an anti-immigration party. There are, as we will see, a handful of other causes that unite Hanson's people. But behind all the complex calculations about what drives people into Hanson's arms, these figures speak with unmistakeable clarity: One Nation voters loathe immigrants. It's an embarrassing challenge for a decent country to find such forces at work, but it is much too late to pretend that a party which displays such extreme hostility to immigration is not driven by race. That's simply not facing facts.

Anger with government

One Nation is the Pissed Off with Government Party. They were so the last time, when Australians still trusted their governments. In those days, being ignored by politicians was the base complaint of the party. Hanson was the gutsy politician who listened. Twenty years later, with trust in government sagging across the country, One Nation is coming into its own as the party that accuses politicians of not listening. It's the brand.

Nothing beats the hostility of Hanson's voters here. This is the party breakdown of those who believe politicians "usually look after themselves":

National	39 per cent
Liberal	40 per cent
Labor	51 per cent
Green	51 per cent
One Nation	85 per cent

McAllister rates this number "real and something worth focusing on." He sees it as a measure of general dissatisfaction, not with government so much as the political class. "This taps into Brexit, Trump, Italy – this disaffection with the political class, that career politicians seem to be looking after their own vested interests and not looking after the interests of ordinary voters."

This is a bigger issue than One Nation. Huntley reports: "The general conversation from the community is that politicians seem like a kind of a club: they all know each other, they all went to university. They see them as highly educated, highly connected, an elite they have never been part of." There's anger across the board at the failure of government to solve problems. "They think 'There are these problems, these problems didn't exist before, governments are responsible, I blame the government.' So part of it is the easiest outlet for anger but also that kind of sense that politicians seem completely remote to them."

Markus ran some figures for me from the Scanlon survey to show what those most angry with government are angry about. Gloom about the economy is clearly linked to dissatisfaction with government. But by far the most dramatic call for a shake-up of the system comes from those angriest about levels of immigration:

	Government:			
	Is working fine	Needs minor change	Needs major change	Needs replacing
Immigration numbers are:				
Too high:	24	25	43	52
About right:	51	47	33	20

Immigration isn't everything in the current stew of discontent. There's so much in there: scandal, logjam, a tepid economy, and the slaughter of prime ministers. But clearly on these numbers the nation's discontent cannot be understood without facing the role played by minority rage over immigration. And the AES figures show no issue so unites One Nation as immigration. McAllister calls it "the touchstone."

Other issues that fire up One Nation voters

Hanson's people are not implacable conservatives. They aren't hostile to unions and they believe – this figure in the AES is quite clear – that big business has too much power. Nor is One Nation preaching family values. They are not lining up against equal marriage. (In focus groups they say: Why not let them get on with it?) Hanson's people are second only to the Greens in wanting marijuana decriminalised: 68 per cent of Greens to 49 per cent of One Nation. Not that they've given up on the War on Drugs. They loathe ice and fear it as a source of crime and violence. And Hanson's people are absolutely of one mind on allowing the terminally ill to end their own lives with medical assistance: support in the party runs at 98 per cent.

On the other hand, Hanson's people are particularly tough on crime. One of her causes back in the late 1990s was the right of parents to spank their children. She believes in the rod. But that's only a start. Here's the breakdown by party of those in 2016 calling for stiffer sentences for law-breakers:

Greens   9 per cent
Labor   24 per cent
Liberal   30 per cent
National   31 per cent
One Nation   50 per cent

And their faith in the gallows is complete. Twenty years ago, when the Member for Oxley stormed into Canberra, there was a strong majority across the community for bringing back the noose for murder. That support has fallen, according to the AES, to 40 per cent. But among One Nation voters, the passion for the death penalty is undiminished:

Greens   15 per cent
Labor   40 per cent
Liberal   42 per cent
National   54 per cent
One Nation   88 per cent

Huntley is struck by the links between One Nation's two agendas: law and order, and immigration. "Where I've worked with people who I know are One Nation voters or highly One Nation–empathetic, they will give absurd examples of their fears. I once met in South Australia this man who was very, very adamant on banning the burqa because he was concerned that large groups of women in their burqas would line up behind him at the ATM and steal his PIN number. But the general way this plays out in groups is for someone to say, 'Once upon a time you could leave your door open' or 'You could go to the pub and put your wallet next to your beer and go to the loo and you'd be surrounded by people just like you, people who would never even think to touch your wallet. But now you can't do that.' A discussion about asylum seekers and immigration will slip very quickly into that sort of talk. There's a really intense nexus between law and order and immigration in that group."

Yearning for the past

Huntley: "Hanson plugs into a range of complaints, most of them complaints that governments can do nothing about. They're the unsolvable complaints, complaints of the modern world. If you live in the modern world, it comes with divorce, it comes with open borders, it comes with refugees. People are nostalgic. If you push most people and say, 'All right, let's go back to the 1950s,' they retreat. They say: 'As much as we like this, as much as we talk about that, do we really want to go back to the world of the six o'clock swill and a world where a woman had to give up her job the moment she got married?' They think beyond the platitudes about how nice it was to live in neighbourhoods where you knew your neighbours and all the rest of it and realise they don't want to go back there. But the One Nation group is genuinely nostalgic. They will genuinely say, 'Yes, I want to go back to that time.' How far back? To the young adulthood of their fathers, which they imagine wasn't so long ago. And they wonder if so much that's happened since couldn't be unravelled. The picture of One Nation is much more complex than the traditional view of them as disaffected, working class, unemployed, the left-behinds from globalisation."

Which parties are Hanson voters deserting?

That answer was straightforward the first time round: some Labor but mostly Coalition. Before the politicians drove Hanson out of parliament, the Coalition was in a world of pain. For every vote Beazley lost, Howard lost two. But the vote in 2016 was more complicated. Here's the AES breakdown:

Previous choice of those who voted One Nation in:	1998	2016
Coalition	53	39
Labor	23	39
Green	3	5
Other (later including PUP)	19	16

First the Palmer United Party collapsed. His was a classic protest party, its supporters not drawn by any policies Clive Palmer was advocating but driven by distaste for Labor and the Coalition. With the PUP perch gone, these voters have largely flown to One Nation. Most of Hanson's vote at the election last year came roughly equally from Labor and the Coalition. That was then. Since her reappearance in Canberra, support for One Nation has blossomed. The most recent polls show her drawing greater backing than ever before. A Newspoll in late February put her support at 10 per cent, more than double her showing at the 2016 election. The Cullerton circus hasn't touched her. Nor have defections, sackings and recriminations inside the party. She's into double figures on a national poll and, for her, that's riding high. There are signs she's winning more of her new following this time at the expense of Labor. Hanson was a spectator sport for Kim Beazley. Not for Shorten.

Does Pauline have legs?

"As a protest vote I would have thought, yes," says McAllister. "In the longer term it depends whether One Nation can basically transition from what is a charismatic party based on one individual through to a pro-grammatic party that's got a stable set of policy issues, and that's the difficult part of it." He watched that transformation with the Greens. It took time. "Labor voters generally were fed up with Labor so they voted Green. They only did it once and then they moved back to Labor. And then what we saw in the last three or four elections was this much greater retention of the Green vote. So it would take a long time for One Nation to transition into something more stable."

Those who see Hanson tapping into something murkier than mere disenchantment with politics fear One Nation will never be dealt with until the major parties find the courage to address the issue that haunts this country: race. Their understanding – it's bipartisan – is that however they try to deal with the drift of votes to One Nation, they cannot afford to denounce Hanson as a racist. "We can only address this through dealing with their economic insecurities," said Labor's Kosmos Samaras. "If you say to someone, 'Vote for us because that woman is racist,' we'd be classified as elites. We'll get killed electorally. If all we do is try to address the cultural issues, we'll lose." Of course, the big parties could try doing both: confront the racism and deal with the economic issues. But that isn't happening. As Turnbull and Shorten shift ground to try to win back One Nation's vote, the R-word scarcely if ever passes their lips.

People listen to Hanson. It's her gift. The only political asset she has is an unshakable belief out there that she speaks for real Australians as no politician can. Fighting her way back to parliament earned her fresh respect. Perseverance is admired in this country. We love a comeback. She's been forgiven the blunders of the past to a remarkable degree. "She went too far back then," they say in focus groups, by which they mean hounding Aboriginals. Putting the boot into Muslims is seen, by contrast, as respectable work. A contradiction is beginning to stare her followers in the face. It doesn't trouble them. She's admired because she's not a politician, while being credited on all sides with becoming more skilled at her work. "She's a lot better now," they say. "She's learnt a lot, she knows what she's doing." And that is politics.

Hanson hesitated to leave prison. At 4.30 that afternoon, watching television in her cell, she heard the Queensland Court of Appeal had overturned her conviction for fraud. "I threw my hands in the air and softly yelled 'YES' to myself." She was free but she had nothing to wear. "I wasn't going to walk out in my prison clothes and let the media see me in my unflattering prison garb." Wacol Prison had racks of clothes for departing prisoners. Hanson looked them over. Nothing. So she waited, a few steps from freedom, for her son to deliver a white crew-neck tank top, black slacks and a pair of black peep-toe shoes. She dressed, signed a few last forms and walked out into the embrace of the television cameras. She looked a million dollars. In a quavering voice she declared: "The system let me down, like it let a lot of people down."

Yes and no.

The facts were not in doubt. In October 1997, Hanson went to the Brisbane office of the state's electoral commissioner, Des O'Shea, to register her party in Queensland. The rules said she had to produce the names of 500 members. She brought a list of over a thousand. Her paperwork was a shambles, but once a couple of hundred people on the list told O'Shea's people they were, indeed, members of Pauline Hanson's One Nation, the party was registered, which made it eligible for public funding. After One Nation's 1998 triumph, two cheques arrived at the party's Ipswich office, totalling $498,637. But there were two problems. First, One Nation did not officially have the 500 members Hanson claimed. It had three: her, Oldfield and Ettridge. The "members" who thought they were members weren't on the books, and the triumvirate running the party knew they weren't when Hanson went down to the commissioner's office that day with her list. That might not have worried anyone much, but for the second problem: Terry Sharples.

Hanson attracts vivid, energetic followers. These men and women may, at times, be difficult to deal with. That's not surprising: without combative

Never again miss an issue. Subscribe and save.

- ☐ **1 year auto-renewing print and digital subscription** (4 issues) $69.95 incl. GST (save 23%). Subscriptions outside Australia $109.95.
- ☐ **1 year print and digital subscription** (4 issues) $79.95 incl. GST (save 13%). Subscriptions outside Australia $119.95.
- ☐ **2 year print and digital subscription** (8 issues) $149.95 incl. GST (save 18%).
- ☐ Tick here to commence subscription with the current issue.

All prices include postage and handling.

PAYMENT DETAILS I enclose a cheque/money order made out to Schwartz Publishing Pty Ltd. Or please debit my credit card (MasterCard, Visa or Amex accepted).

CARD NO. ☐☐☐☐ ☐☐☐☐ ☐☐☐☐ ☐☐☐☐

EXPIRY DATE   /   CCV   AMOUNT $

CARDHOLDER'S NAME

SIGNATURE

NAME

ADDRESS

EMAIL   PHONE

Freecall: 1800 077 514 **or** +61 3 9486 0288 **email:** subscribe@quarterlyessay.com **quarterlyessay.com**
Digital-only subscriptions are available from our website: quarterlyessay.com.au/subscribe

An inspired gift. Subscribe a friend.

- ☐ **1 year print and digital subscription** (4 issues) $79.95 incl. GST (save 13%). Subscriptions outside Australia $119.95.
- ☐ **2 year print and digital subscription** (8 issues) $149.95 incl. GST (save 18%).
- ☐ Tick here to commence subscription with the current issue.

All prices include postage and handling.

PAYMENT DETAILS I enclose a cheque/money order made out to Schwartz Publishing Pty Ltd. Or please debit my credit card (MasterCard, Visa or Amex accepted).

CARD NO. ☐☐☐☐ ☐☐☐☐ ☐☐☐☐ ☐☐☐☐

EXPIRY DATE   /   CCV   AMOUNT $

CARDHOLDER'S NAME   SIGNATURE

NAME

ADDRESS

EMAIL   PHONE

RECIPIENT'S NAME

RECIPIENT'S ADDRESS

RECIPIENT'S EMAIL   PHONE

Freecall: 1800 077 514 **or** +61 3 9486 0288 **email:** subscribe@quarterlyessay.com **quarterlyessay.com**
Digital-only subscriptions are available from our website: quarterlyessay.com.au/subscribe

Delivery Address:
LEVEL 1, 221 DRUMMOND ST
CARLTON VIC 3053

Quarterly Essay
REPLY PAID 90094
CARLTON VIC 3053

Delivery Address:
LEVEL 1, 221 DRUMMOND ST
CARLTON VIC 3053

No stamp required
if posted in Australia

Quarterly Essay
REPLY PAID 90094
CARLTON VIC 3053

instincts, why would they throw themselves into the work of One Nation? Hanson feeds off their energy in the good times, but when the going gets rough they can turn on her. It's the pattern of her career: odd personalities gravitate to her, but if she falls out with them – as she so often has over the years – they make her life hell. Disgruntlement is a familiar issue in the history of One Nation.

Sharples was an accountant who volunteered to contest the seat of Burleigh. He paid his $40 membership fee and a card came in the post a few days later saying he was member 6227 of Pauline Hanson's One Nation. He fell out swiftly with Oldfield. He didn't win the seat. When head office refused to reimburse Sharples for his expenses, he decided to sue. He then discovered the oddest thing: despite his membership card, he wasn't a member. He sniffed a fraud. A few weeks after the election, Tony Abbott gave Sharples a grossly unwise personal guarantee to cover his out-of-pocket expenses in the litigation. Armed with the guarantee, Sharples went to the Queensland Supreme Court a couple of days later to have One Nation in Queensland deregistered. The case made a splash. Abbott – at this point a mere parliamentary secretary to the Minister for Employment, Education, Training and Youth Affairs – lied about the deal to Tony Jones on *Four Corners*:

> JONES: So there was never any question of any party funds—
> ABBOTT: Absolutely not.
> JONES: Or other funds from any other source—
> ABBOTT: Absolutely not.
> JONES: Being offered to Terry Sharples?
> ABBOTT: Absolutely not.

When his lie was exposed years later, Abbott was unrepentant. He told the *Sydney Morning Herald*'s Deborah Snow: "How else were we going to stop One Nation at the time? Who else was fighting against One Nation?"

Sharples brought the hidden structure of One Nation to light in the Brisbane courts in early 1999. All those "members" who thought they had signed up to the party had – unknown to them – been shuffled into the Pauline Hanson Support Group. This wasn't a secret inside the organisation. Ettridge and Oldfield explained to a number of party intimates what this was about: making sure no one but the triumvirate had any say in the running of the party. It seemed they feared the Yellow Peril:

> Mr Ettridge and Mr Oldfield scoffed at the idea that members of the Chinese community would be able to join Pauline Hanson's One Nation in sufficient numbers to have her removed because they had total control and no-one would be able to remove them or Ms Hanson.

Ettridge told Andrew Carne, who set up One Nation's database: "We are not a political party – a party is where you wear funny hats and have balloons and streamers – and that is what makes us different." A number of "members" also knew about the peculiar structure of One Nation. Peter Archer of Newcastle was not happy about it: "When Mr Archer opined that the party structure was not democratic, Mr Ettridge replied that he did not believe in democracy."

The party was deregistered in Queensland in August 1999. Justice Roslyn Atkinson of the Queensland Supreme Court found:

> Those members of management committee involved in the application for registration, being Ms Hanson and Mr Ettridge, must have known that Pauline Hanson's One Nation had no members except themselves and Mr Oldfield and so they induced the registration by their fraud and misrepresentation.

Hanson and Ettridge had to hand back the half million dollars of public funding. Hanson opened a Fighting Fund to make good the loss, and donations flooded in. But her troubles were far from over. In July 2001 she and Ettridge were charged with electoral fraud, and the following year Hanson was charged with dipping into the Fighting Fund to pay an American Express bill and buy her daughter a car. (These latter charges were dropped.) In August 2003, after twenty-three days and thirty witnesses, a district court jury found both guilty of fraud. Judge Patricia Wolfe sentenced them to three years' imprisonment, in order, she said, that the electoral processes of Queensland not be thwarted or perverted. The prisoners were taken down. Hanson wrote: "I felt the cold, heavy handcuffs being placed on my wrists."

This was a brutal fate for an upstart politician who seemed, in any case, absolutely washed up. Oldfield had quit One Nation after spending over a million dollars of party funds to win a place in the NSW Legislative Council. Ettridge walked. Without a seat Hanson had lost all authority in the snake pit of her party. She walked in early 2002. A year later, waiting for her trial to begin, she went south looking for a seat in the NSW upper house. Her campaign was a fiasco. She preached law and order but couldn't name the police chief. She said: "You have to realise that I am from Queensland." Her third defeat in a row provoked fresh obituaries. The *Daily Telegraph*'s Malcolm Farr called this "the final fizz of a political firecracker."

Hanson was behind bars for eleven weeks before the Queensland Court of Appeal rode to her rescue. Chief Justice Paul de Jersey birched her "inexperienced trial counsel" for not coming up with the sophisticated argument he now used to unlock her cell door. What the party leaders thought they were doing didn't matter a bit, said de Jersey. By taking membership fees and issuing membership cards, they were contracting to admit people to membership of Pauline Hanson's One Nation. That this didn't square with the party rules was likewise irrelevant. All the applicants for membership had to do, it seemed, was pop down to the court with a QC to enforce their rights. While de Jersey didn't quibble with the deregistration of the party – Hanson would never get the money back – he ordered the convictions be quashed, "and because a retrial would in the circumstances be futile, judgments and verdicts of acquittal entered." She was free, having acquired – at some cost – a protective badge of martyrdom.

Never believe Hanson if she declares her political life over. She's usually back on the hustings within six months. After Wacol she let it be known politics was behind her, but she was on television before the year was out telling Andrew Denton she would be standing for the Senate in 2004. "I want to be me. I don't want all the hangers-onners. I don't want the advisers and everyone else. I want it to be this time Pauline Hanson." Was there ever such a campaign in the history of Australian politics? She was on the stump in towns up and down Queensland while doing the cha-cha with 24-year-old Latin dance champion Salvatore Vecchio on Channel 7's *Dancing with the Stars*. That it was so tawdry didn't harm her at all. These years of performing on television and touring casinos in song-and-dance shows would make her seem a harmless, comic version of her old political self. Showbiz washed her sins away. She earned a fresh reputation for bravery: this time for facing audiences with so little talent. She craved the attention. Her business was politics, and becoming a celebrity was good for business. The spotlight and the crowds, a new man and an election to fight pumped fresh life into her. Life and cash.

Howard led his government to a great victory in October 2004. Hanson tallied up her fourth defeat. She had no program, just old complaints and dire warnings about the fate of nations divided. The *Age* reported:

> She said she stood for "a way of life that's Australian," and the rural sector that had been crippled by imports. "I see the Australian farmer being destroyed."
>
> Rights that had been fought for by the unions were now being taken away by big conglomerates "that are just there for the profits and the shareholders."
>
> China was "flooding the world with all their products," she said. "We used to have a manufacturing industry base that created jobs, but we've seen these go offshore." Australian icons were now foreign owned.
>
> "There's a lot to be done ... we've got to rebuild Australia."

The strategy of the major parties held: they all preferenced against her. Even so, she won the best vote ever for an independent with a name below the line on the ballot paper. Her 4.5 per cent of the vote in Queensland delivered her — personally — public funding of $199,886.

She had ceased attacking Indigenous Australians. There are those who say she lost her taste for it after coming to know many Indigenous prisoners in Wacol. But in any case, outright abuse of Aboriginal people had become too toxic for any politician to survive. The game now called for skills she couldn't muster. The mining industry was quietly negotiating deals with native-title holders. Money was no longer being pumped into think-tank controversies about cannibalism and genocide. Politicians needed to find more subtle ways of exploiting the big constituency — about a third of the nation according to the AES — that continued to believe government help for the Indigenous was too generous and land rights had gone too far. John Howard knew how to do it. He went on attacking "black armband" historians and resolutely refused to apologise to the Stolen Generations. He would stage the Intervention in the Northern Territory as a curtain-raiser for the 2007 election. This was race politics played by a master.

Hanson took a different course. The week she announced she was running again in 2007 she gave a series of torrid interviews attacking Muslims. Her idea of a fair and just Australia would see all Muslim immigration ended. Headscarves would be banned. Australians already faced a wave of Muslim crime:

> Young boys were caught urinating on the bible, and others rape our young women because they are considered a meat market by some of their leaders.

Muslims would no longer be helped to undermine our way of life:

> Our governments have bent over backwards to look after them and their needs and regardless of what the Australian people think. You can't have schools not sing Christmas carols because it upsets others. You can't close swimming baths because Muslim women want to swim in private. That's not Australian.

And Africans would be stopped from bringing hideous diseases into the country:

> We're bringing in people from South Africa at the moment. There's a huge amount coming into Australia who have diseases; they've got AIDS ... They are of no benefit to this country whatsoever. They'll never be able to work.

There was little time left. The unity of the country was at stake. She urged Queenslanders not to "cast aside the sacrifices given in death and despair by those who fought for our freedom" and vote one Pauline Hanson's United Australia Party. She had registered that party in order to get her name above the line on the ballot paper. She published a campaign memoir, *Untamed and Unashamed*, which created a helpful buzz by revealing her brief affair with Oldfield years before. She gave a DNA swab that revealed her bloodlines included a good deal of Mediterranean and 9 per cent Middle Eastern. She declared herself mystified. Despite all this, her vote retreated a little. Even so, the cheque from Canberra rose to $213,095.

There was trouble over the money. The party's treasurer, Bribie Island businessman Graham McDonald, was furious to discover that Hanson had withdrawn the money from the party's account and paid it into another. The federal police were called. A telephone call with McDonald was taped: "I haven't put all this bloody hard work in to hand control over to it," Hanson said. "I'm not putting the money in the hands of anyone else. I'm not going to go begging. I haven't even drawn any money out of the account myself as yet. My bills are still there. There's nothing illegal about it. It's not going to happen to me again. I'm not going to be out there just pushing the wheelbarrow for everyone else." The spat blew over. No charges were laid. The party was wound up.

Every other year she was back on the campaign trail. How she survived without a job is a mystery. The fish and chip shop was a long time behind her. Of course, she was always good with money. At one point she spoke of having an interest in a country pub. There were investment properties.

But in any case, politics was her business now. Her sense of mission was huge. Everything else aside, Hanson sees herself as *necessary* for Australia.

In Queensland in 2009 she stood as an independent in the seat of Beaudesert, in a far corner of which sat her dream home on the hill. Television cameras swarmed. She denied being in the game for money. "Would you consider that Abraham Lincoln was also a professional candidate?" she asked journalists one day in the streets of Boonah. "I'd suggest you go and have a look up at the number of times that Abraham Lincoln stood for parliament to stand up for what you believe in." The last days of the campaign turned to farce when News Limited published a set of photographs said to be of a naked and cavorting Hanson. They weren't. Experts pointed to the nose. "The young woman's nasal bridge is high, prominent and projecting, and more narrow," observed forensic anatomist Dr Meiya Sutisno of the University of Technology, Sydney. "Pauline Hanson's nasal bridge is quite wide and thick." Hanson sued. Despite everything, she won 22 per cent of the vote in Beaudesert and (under new Queensland rules) a modest $8000 reimbursement of her electoral expenses.

Once again she declared her political life over. This time she spoke of moving to Britain but, after flying over to take a look, changed her mind: "It's overrun with immigrants and refugees." She hunkered down in a new house with a new man in Port Stephen on the north coast of New South Wales and made a second run in 2011 for the state's Legislative Council. She tearfully informed the press: "Australia needs me." The media were rather bored. Without preferences her 2.4 per cent of the vote did not win her a seat. To her fury, a couple of candidates with even fewer primary votes slipped past her at the finish. She challenged the result in court and lost. She was furious. The campaign cost her over $100,000 and she got nothing back. She said: "I think the government needs to have a look at the voting system."

Glenn Druery had once more seen to her defeat. The man they called the "preference whisperer" had organised against her at nearly every poll since establishing his Minor Party Alliance in 1999. He loathed Hanson's attacks on blacks and Muslims, and feared the damage she might do to the nation. So he mustered the minor parties to join the major parties preferencing against her. He spoke of it as a "public service" he performed free of charge. Druery had a far more Machiavellian plan in mind for the 2013 poll: he would persuade Hanson to rejoin One Nation and draw the party into his alliance. He would then direct the votes she raised to other little parties. In effect, he would pool and wash them. Other voices were also urging Hanson to come back to the fold. A couple of party stalwarts – Ian Nelson and Jim Savage – bent on reviving the party's fortunes also worked on her to rejoin. Between them all, they persuaded Hanson to go back to the party she had left a decade before and stand for the Senate under its banner. Her prospects seemed bright. There was much press chatter of phoenixes rising from the ashes. Druery's role seemed to bode well for Hanson. The *Canberra Times* reported:

> The One Nation founder's Senate bid is being engineered by Glenn Druery. Mr Druery is a political deal-maker who specialises in getting right-leaning minor parties into Parliament through carefully orchestrated preference swaps ... The Greens and the Shooters and Fishers Party, which are vying for the last Senate seat in NSW along with Ms Hanson and the Liberal Party, believe Mr Druery has stitched up a deal that will put Ms Hanson in a competitive position even without preferences from the two main parties.

Not quite. Druery knew her chances were better in Queensland, so he persuaded her to stand in New South Wales. Then luck took his side: Hanson drew a terrible position on the ballot paper. The ABC's man, Antony Green, ran the sums: Hanson and Howard's former chief of staff, Arthur Sinodinos, would be vying to become the state's sixth senator.

Abbott had lost none of his antagonism to Hanson. At a press conference in a Sydney police station the leader of the Opposition announced One Nation was among "one or two parties that are frankly racist" which the Coalition would be preferencing last. Her message certainly hadn't changed. Out of her mouth came a stream of local gripes infused with race hate: wind farms and tariffs, welfare cheats and asylum seekers, 457 visas and foreign ownership, multiculturalism and Muslims. But asked one day at a careers expo in Western Sydney if her attitude to Asians had changed since she was last in parliament, she replied: "Yes, they have, because that was 15, 16, 17 years ago." When the writer Benjamin Law quizzed her further, she babbled. "You've got to have a balance, otherwise you have a dominating culture. I suppose I'm a proud Australian! I don't want to see my culture gone. Does anyone?" And there was the curious sight of her utter delight at being mobbed by multicultural Australia:

> Women in hijabs shake Hanson's hand; an Indian woman in a sari wishes Hanson the best. Lebanese men, Anglo teens, Chinese women, they all approach Hanson with smiles and smartphones. Someone offers her a free blow-dry. Part of me suspects some of these shoppers are only posing with Hanson for the same reason they'd pose with Queensland's Big Pineapple – it's there – but it's obvious many of them adore Hanson and her politics.

Yet it was not enough. Green had calculated she stood a chance if she won only 2 per cent of the vote. She got a humiliating 1.1 per cent. The 2013 defeat yielded her not a dollar of public money. That she could fight on after this speaks to something admirable in her character: raw resilience.

She had taken to Facebook with immense enthusiasm. She saw its possibilities at once. She courted cameras and reporters but loathed being questioned. She saw how Facebook could deliver her message without her having to brave the demands and the mockery of the press. In June 2013 she launched her Facebook page, Pauline Hanson's Please Explain. Newsletters were finished. Meetings were almost things of the past. Her message arrived unbidden in the inboxes of the friends of the friends of her friends. She now has 193,000 followers – quite a figure given they are not, by age and education, natural enthusiasts of the internet. They all watch television. In early 2014, having appeared on Sunrise from time to

time for years, she was signed up by Channel 7 as a regular paid commentator on the show. This is the perch the obscure Kevin Rudd used to
make himself a big political figure across Australia. The mix was a little
different for Hanson. But from early 2014 she was always there on
Monday mornings with something tart to say about schools, housing,
political correctness, flag burning, vaccinations, apprenticeships and the
perpetual threat of Muslim violence. When she once again took the helm
of her party in November 2014, Sunrise was her platform to announce she
was changing the name back to Pauline Hanson's One Nation:

> Don't get me wrong about this. This is nothing to do with an ego.
> I have no ego. I have always said in the past if anyone came along
> that can do a better job than I can, please do it, because my heart is
> with the country. But I think that people relate to me because a lot
> of the issues and policies are how I feel and it's come from me. So
> I think the party is me.

She had a last defeat in her. At the poll that saw Campbell Newman's
LNP government swept from power in early 2015, Hanson stood in the
seat of Lockyer in the hinterland of Ipswich. Hanson had broken with
Glenn Druery. They exchanged insults. She said: "He is untrustworthy and
does deals behind the scenes and you never know who he is really working for." He said: "Pauline's comments don't bother me – she is yesterday's
woman." Lockyer was promising territory: in the glory days of One Nation
the seat had returned a couple of members to the Brisbane parliament. The
times also suited her: these were the weeks immediately after the slaughter
in the Lindt Café. She didn't have to say a thing, the message was in the
air. And she came closer than ever: a swing of 23 per cent left her only 114
votes short of unseating the LNP's long-time man in the seat, Ian Rickuss.
One Nation earned public funding of $53,033. There was a curious sight
on polling day: taking photographs for Hanson was the perky gay nemesis
of the former Speaker of the House of Representatives, Peter Slipper. James
Ashby told the Courier-Mail it was "just a one-day thing."

Hanson's people know she is talking race. They talk about it themselves in focus groups. Her candour on race is fundamental to their respect for her. They fear being branded racists if they complain about burqas and mosques and schools forbidding Christmas. She is not afraid. Nothing so establishes her bona fides in their eyes than the courage she shows denouncing blacks and Muslims. Not that they see her as a racist. Not now, anyway. Focus group leaders tell me there's a sense among One Nation voters that Hanson went a bit far in the old days attacking Aborigines and Asians. But she's on the money with Muslims. "We're not racist," they say. "We support Asians. We like them. We think they've done a lot here." But they don't like Muslims. They don't talk bombs and terrorist attacks in focus groups, though perhaps the threat of violence is somewhere in their minds. They talk a bit about lost jobs and a lot about people not fitting in. Not even trying to fit in. One leader of these groups told me: "You hear this complaint in Queensland, but in Western Sydney it's more in your face."

I've come to think it's not much use asking if Australia is a racist country. It's too broadbrush. The better question is: what role does race play in the politics of the country? This is not the politics of class or the politics of money, but the politics of difference. It's pursued in the name of unity and has as its immediate effect division. To many, these divisions are deeply gratifying. They isolate and disempower. Far from putting the survival of the country at risk, they keep things under control. They are a brake on change. The politics of race reassures white Australians unsure of their place in the heap that they're on the only heap that matters. But that doesn't make every last one of them a racist. After a career investigating the workings of race in Australia, Andrew Markus distinguishes between citizens with everyday worries – a mosque being built down the road and the local primary school not celebrating Christmas – and the ideologues.

Hanson has a simple definition of racist: "A person who believes their race to be superior to another's." She claims that's not her. Never was. She says she has never advocated the superiority of her race over others. "I challenge anyone to tell me one thing that I've said that is racist. Criticism is not racism. Accountability is not racism." She bills herself as the voice of worried citizens, the protectress of the Australian way of life. Yet though her career may have begun with a folksy distaste for the blacks of Ipswich, she has grown over time into an ideologue of race, one of those with what Markus sees as the distinguishing mark of a racist: a conspiratorial mindset.

At her election in 1996 race moved close to the centre of national politics. Howard's neutering of her was technically masterful. His alliance with her people was a key element in his survival for a decade in power. As Australia weathered the opening of its economy to the world, he offered reassurance to vulnerable Australians on race, sex (keeping things heterosexual in the *Marriage Act*), religion, the monarchy, and smut on the screen. These years saw the last gasp of official censorship, about to be rendered pointless by the internet. Then in 2001, the focus of race politics narrowed sharply with the demolition of the World Trade Center. The Bali bombings the following year intensified this. We were close to the people who died in that nightclub. Fear entered the equation. Fear of invasion by boat people was already part of race politics. But this was more potent: fear of Muslims.

We didn't know any. Except in a couple of suburbs in a couple of cities, Muslims were complete strangers to us. Whatever the term might mean in the outside world, Australians used Muslim to mean Egyptians, Lebanese, all Arabs, Iranians and Pakistanis. Faith and race, in this coarse analysis, were interchangeable. Television brought news of terrible things perpetrated by Muslim fanatics abroad. Australians were particularly affected by the London bombings of 2005. Months later a riot broke out in the Sydney suburb of Cronulla, a familiar turf brawl on the beach with a new and violent race twist. Anglo thugs waved Australian flags as they beat Middle Eastern boys while shouting: "Love Nulla, Fuck Allah."

Among those revving up that riot was the doyen of talkback, Alan Jones. Howard refused to condemn the riots. "I do not accept that there is underlying racism in this country," he said. "I have always taken a more optimistic view of the Australian people." Hanson blamed the police for not making enough arrests – her count was wildly wrong – and the media for once again missing the story: "They cover up how Aussies feel about issues, they protect the migrants and they sensationalised the story and sent the wrong message to the rest of the world." Cronulla didn't drive her back to politics. The riot fell in the long gap of three years she filled with appearances on talk shows and the fruitless pursuit of the half-million dollars taken from her when she went to jail. But when she did return to politics in late 2006 she had a new message and that was the evil of Islam. She wasn't voicing everyday fears. She began pursuing, campaign by campaign, a deeply ideological attack on Islam.

"Islam is proving to be seditious against every nation and government on earth," declares One Nation's Islam policy. "Islam demands that all Muslims work to overthrow all nations, governments and non-sharia laws." The trustworthiness of even non-religious Muslims in our midst is put in doubt: "If Jihad is called (applying any methods, including threats, deceit and ISIS-style warfare, to establish Islam as the dominant power, completely endorsed by Allah and Mohammed) where do their loyalties lie?" Halal certification is a $10-million-a-year "racket." The imposition of sharia law seems just around the corner. And viewed properly, Islam isn't a faith but a totalitarian ideology. "Its religious aspect is a fraud." This truly zany idea doesn't get the attention it deserves. Philip Dorling in a splendid paper for the Australia Institute, "The American Far-Right Origins of Pauline Hanson's Views on Islam," writes: "To claim that Islam is not actually a religion [is] a novel proposition even within the far right-wing fringe of Australian politics." But in America it serves a particular purpose for ruthless Christian warriors like radio evangelist Pat Robertson and talk-show host Rush Limbaugh. "How could they square their love of freedom with their desire to clamp down on one particular religion?"

asked Dorling. "So about a decade ago, a new idea arose in conservative Christian circles: Islam is not a religion." The far right lapped up the idea that this faith of billions deserved no protection under the US constitution. The notion was picked up by Team Trump. Ben Carson, now US Secretary for Housing and Urban Development, has signed on. Geert Wilders is a believer. Dorling argues that Hanson:

> is singing from their hymn sheet. In her approach to Islam and religious freedom she is channelling some of the more extreme aspects of American far right politics into the Australian political landscape ... many other elements of One Nation's outlook and policies – for example, its attacks on the United Nations and the Agenda 21 sustainable development action plan – have their origins in American far-right thinking and activism. It is likely that One Nation will continue to draw much inspiration and adopt ideas and policies from the US 'alt-right' for some time to come.

A few months ago, Hanson had lunch with Dr Anne Aly. "She literally said to me, 'Oh, but Anne, you're not a real Muslim because you aren't advocating to throw people off buildings or behead people.'" Aly is an authority on radicalisation, a Muslim and the Labor member for the Perth seat of Cowan. "I said to her, 'Pauline, can you understand that most Muslims are like me and can you understand how much more difficult you make it for us by saying those people aren't real Muslims?'" Aly's sense is that Hanson isn't really concerned about Muslims. "They don't factor into it at all. It's about homing in on those fears that people in Australia have. She's manipulated those fears for twenty years – whether it's the fear of being swamped by Asians or the fear of being swamped by Muslims. It is homing in on those fears that matters the most." Do you think she's driven by genuine fears, I asked, or do you think she knows she's on a winner? "I think she knows she's on a winner."

Aly sees two kinds of Hanson supporters. "There are disaffected voters who honestly think she's saying the things that nobody else wants to say, and they are really attracted by her rhetoric of holding the government to account. They're the ones who are starting to become very disillusioned with the fact that she's made deals with the Liberals, that she votes with the Liberals on everything, she's voted to cut pensions, all of those things. So they're the ones who are not necessarily attracted to her anti-Muslim rhetoric but who are attracted to that rebellious nature of hers in the hope that she can hold politics to account. The others don't really give two hoots about any of her other policies. They are particularly attracted to her anti-Muslim and anti-immigration stance and everything else falls by the wayside. They're the ones who, for example, will vote for a candidate who has been exposed as a crackpot who believes in Nazi mind control and things like that."

Aly agrees with Markus that there's a hardcore (he says 14 per cent of the population) that's clearly hostile towards Muslims and an outer periphery (he says another 10 per cent) that holds vaguer fears of Islam. "Those people talk about feminism all the time and how they're protecting feminism and that's why they're against Islam," says Aly. "But you know they'd step over a woman who's been beaten by her husband tomorrow." Aly points to a particular group within the deeply hostile: "The rabid white supremacist groups who have flocked to Pauline Hanson. They're not just anti-Muslim. They're also anti-Semitic, they're homophobic, and they're a whole range of other things as well." And Hanson, she argues, has become an icon for anti-Muslims. "She's become this receptacle of an entire country's fears and an entire country's angst – even, at the most crude level, racism." She doubts Hanson's followers ever look at what she actually has to say about Islam. "One of the things that made me laugh is that she's proposing these obligatory prenuptials. That's Sharia."

Race politics are changing Muslim Australia. "Younger generations of Muslims have adopted Islam as their primary identity marker. If you talk to people my age, they'll say, oh, 'I'm Lebanese' or 'I'm Egyptian' or 'I'm Iraqi' or whatever. Our primary identity marker was our ethnicity. After 9/11 you had a lot of young Australian Muslims stand up and say, 'I'm

Muslim.' In the post-9/11 world we didn't really equip them with the skills for dealing with what is essentially a conflict zone – a cultural conflict more than anything else – and I think using Islam as their primary identity marker is being defensive and being part of something bigger that they can relate to. If they're no longer Australian, or they're consistently told that they're no longer Australian, they have to be something." She remembers a few years ago a focus group of young Muslim men in tears saying, "I always considered myself Australian and then suddenly I've been told I'm not Australian."

"If Trump is 'Make America Great Again,' Pauline is 'Keep Australia Anxious.' The level of anxiety is not in touch with reality but keeps us in this state of constant dread that is very easily manipulated in the Australian imagination. I think that's what we're talking about here: the Australian imagination. How do we imagine ourselves?" Aly sees a nation vulnerable to fears of invasion. "We've always felt endangered. We've always felt endangered from the first moment that white settlers stepped a foot on this country." And from the start that fear has been manipulated. "Sometimes it bubbles below the surface and sometimes it spills over the top and you've got to wonder at what point do we as a society go, enough! Two hundred years. Come on, people, move on."

Tony Abbott has never shown much enthusiasm for free speech. He hadn't worried about censorship and secrecy in the Howard years. He's always denounced the idea of Australia having a Bill of Rights. He never worked for the reform of Australia's notorious defamation laws. But as leader of the Opposition he became an enthusiastic campaigner to save Australia from section 18C of the *Racial Discrimination Act*. He wasn't disturbed by laws that protected the old, the queer or the disabled from abuse. But he wanted 18C gutted so the law set no effective brake on racial vilification in public discourse. There was more to this than vindicating his old supporter Andrew Bolt. This was about persuading a chunk of the electorate that once in power Abbott would lead a government after their own hearts: one that understands what they feel about Aborigines, immigrants, boat people and Muslims; a government that would let them vent. Hanson was one of those people. She once told Andrew Denton:

> What annoys me so much is the Australian people are being suppressed in their views and their opinions by policies and legislation set down by our so-called parliamentarians. Why the hell did they bring in a racial and religious vilification law that shuts Australians down from having an opinion? I have a right to have an opinion. But I'm being shut down.

Denton observed dryly: "I would suggest you're one of the least shutdown people I've ever seen." That was always the problems for critics of 18C: proving it stifled debate. Where were the martyrs? Who was being punished for speech that might, in the words of the Act, "offend, insult, humiliate or intimidate" people because of their "race, colour or national or ethnic origin"?

Then along came Andrew Bolt and the columns he wrote in the *Herald Sun* in 2009 attacking "professional" Aborigines who could pass for white but choose to identify as black for personal or for political gain, to win prizes and take what belonged to real, black Aborigines. Here's Bolt on the academic Larissa Behrendt:

> She's won many positions and honours as an Aborigine, including the David Unaipon Award for Indigenous Writers, and is often interviewed demanding special rights for "my people." But which people are "yours," exactly, mein liebchen? And isn't it bizarre to demand laws to give you more rights as a white Aborigine than your own white dad?

Meaty stuff. But Bolt had his facts hopelessly wrong. At least nine of the "White Aborigines" he ridiculed in his columns hadn't switched race to get ahead. Like Behrendt, they were raised black. Her father was not a German but a black Australian. She had identified as black from before she could remember. The nine he abused chose not to sue Bolt. They did not want damages, but a correction and a promise he would not print such rubbish again. So they brought an action under the *Racial Discrimination Act*. Even before it went to court, Bolt had to admit he was wrong about the lot of them. He went down for his errors, compounded by his insults. But he emerged from the Federal Court in late 2011 giving a creditable impersonation of a martyr for free speech. Abbott leapt to his defence and won office promising to get rid of 18C.

But he gave up after less than a year. This was a key moment in race politics in this country. It set the ground rules. Abbott's plan had not won public backing. But more to the point, the notion of gutting the *Racial Discrimination Act* had infuriated the Jewish, Chinese, Greek, Armenian and Muslim communities. "If we had battled on against 18C," one senior Liberal told me, "they would have torn us apart." Their anger brought home to party leaders what their pollsters had been saying for some time: the Liberal Party couldn't survive as a mainstream movement representing only white Australia. Its future is multicultural. Antagonising Indians and Chinese would be reckless. Many among them are natural Liberal voters. So Abbott beat a humiliating retreat on

18C, covering it as best he could by claiming the withdrawal was necessary for the security of the country: "When it comes to counter-terrorism, everyone needs to be part of Team Australia," he said. "The government's perfectly-reasonable-under-different-circumstances attempt to amend section 18C has become a complication that we just don't need and we're not going to proceed with."

Yet playing for the anti-Muslim vote continued. By this time, hardly anyone was left within the party who found this distasteful. The Howard years had seen the end of the influence of the liberal Liberals – not least because Howard had tied the party to a refugee policy hitherto unthinkable for that side of politics. Events in Abbott's time as prime minister gave those who despised Islam a great deal to work with: terrorist attacks in France, Australians fighting with ISIS (aka Daesh) in the Middle East, terror plots thwarted at home, a stabbing in Victoria, and – whether or not this is to be counted as terrorism or lunacy – the Martin Place siege in Sydney. Abbott fancied himself as a pocket Churchill. His rhetoric was apocalyptic: "As far as the Daesh death cult is concerned, it's coming after us." He insulted Jewish leaders by declaring Daesh worse than the Nazis: "The Nazis did terrible evil but they had a sufficient sense of shame to try to hide it. These people boast about their evil . . ." A few days after the first challenge to his leadership in early 2015, he brutally goaded Muslims: "I've often heard Western leaders describe Islam as a 'religion of peace'. I wish more Muslim leaders would say that more often, and mean it." At this point the head of the Arab Council Australia, Randa Kattan, accused the prime minister of "promoting hatred and inflaming racism." Abbott was undeterred. For a politician who spent so much of his energy whipping up scare campaigns, he proved curiously unable to profit by them. He had frightened his way into government, but once there seemed not to understand the rules of the game: after you scare, you reassure. It's the reassurance that wins votes. In the end Australians didn't buy his vision of a nation in peril, nor were we persuaded that having him at the helm guaranteed our safety.

Hanson surprised no one by announcing, soon after Lockyer, that she would stand for the Senate in Queensland in 2016. There was nothing nuanced about the last lap of her long journey back to Canberra: she flayed Islam up and down the country. She posted on Facebook: "A vote for me at the next Federal Election will be your insurance, the major parties will have absolute opposition to any more Mosques, Sharia Law, Halal Certification & Muslim Refugees. NO MORE! Share if you agree." That post was shared 37,000 times. She ignored denials by the Australian Federal Police and the Australian Crime Commission and continued to peddle the myth that halal certification was financing terrorism. After the slaughter in Paris in November 2015 she appeared with furrowed brows on *Sunrise* and *Today* demanding the country be closed to Muslims: "People of Australia don't want more Muslim refugees in Australia who may be ISIS plants. Protect and give the Australian people the security they need and are screaming out for." She had never had such an audience. Within a few days that clip was viewed over two million times and her next post – "RELIGION OF 'PEACE' CLAIMS 118 LIVES" – brought One Nation 16,000 fresh followers.

She was stealing everyone's thunder. Her name was her brand. That she spouted hate and her sentences were all over the shop didn't matter. Pauline was the one the media went to. Putting a camera in her face guaranteed something worth watching. None of the far-right outfits that sprang into existence after the Martin Place siege won anything like the attention she did. Reclaim Australia – an alliance of anti-Islam activists, including some ugly neo-Nazi thugs – made the news with violent clashes in Melbourne at its launch at Easter 2015, but Hanson was the star of the Brisbane rally that day. "Muslims were seen dancing and celebrating on the streets of Sydney" after 9/11, she told a crowd in King George Square. And absent swift action, sharia law was about to descend on Australia:

> Do you honestly want to see the legal age for marriage lowered to
> nine for little girls? Do you want to see hands and feet cut off as a

form of punishment? Do you want to see young girls going through female genital mutilation? Do you want to see homosexuals sentenced to death? Do you want to see marriage without consent?

The Dutch campaigner against Islam, Geert Wilders, made a bit of a splash when he came to launch an outfit called the Australian Liberty Alliance. But the cameras returned to Hanson. It was worth it every time.

Then Abbott fell. The country was thrilled to see a modern man become prime minister. Turnbull was sharp. He had a sense of humour. He'd had a life before politics. He seemed to stand above old brawls and promise the country a bright future. He didn't breathe fear. In *Still Lucky*, her beautiful account of her years spent exploring Australia through hundreds of focus groups, Rebecca Huntley recalls the country becoming tired of Abbott and ready to switch to Turnbull.

> The installation of Malcolm Turnbull gave the Australian public something more valuable, arguably, than any one policy or spending promise. It meant the end of a period of intense embarrassment and the restoration of some national pride … In all kinds of groups I conducted in the months after the Liberal Party spill, the relief was palpable … In the discussion groups, there was something amounting almost to euphoria over Turnbull's ascension.

Not among Hanson's people. The national secretary of One Nation, Saraya Beric, told the *Australian* the phones didn't stop ringing after Abbott was deposed. "They are Liberal members and lifetime voters who will never vote for them under Turnbull."

Hanson had a problem: the police were investigating her new *consigliere*, James Ashby. The young man sighted on polling day in Lockyer had become indispensable to her operation. He had a pilot's licence and a printing business on the Gold Coast. Both were put to work for One Nation. He was a whizzkid with social media. With Ashby around, a new note of professionalism had crept into Hanson's operation. In his early months with her he told the *Australian*: "I am only dipping my toe back into the political waters. I want to help Pauline out and don't see this as a major step to the extreme Right." His problems with the police were a hangover from the brutal destruction of his old employer, the renegade Speaker, Peter Slipper. Ashby's claim that the old man was sexually harassing him found no traction until he took it to Mal Brough. It was an odd course to take: instead of confronting Slipper; instead of appealing to the officers of parliament; instead of finding himself a lawyer; instead of going to the police, he brought his complaint to Slipper's sworn political enemy. Slipper was done for, but Brough had left Ashby with a problem. On 60 *Minutes*, under the penetrating gaze of Liz Hayes, he was foolishly candid. "Did you ask James Ashby to procure copies of Peter Slipper's diary for you?" she asked. "Yes, I did," he replied. Labor called in the Australian Federal Police. While a good many people – even inside the Coalition – were delighted by the prospect of Brough brought undone, the immediate focus of police inquiries was Ashby. He was the "Commonwealth officer" who may have breached section 70 of the *Crimes Act* by the unauthorised disclosure of Slipper's diary. Penalty: imprisonment for two years. Ashby denied any wrongdoing.

Ashby, meanwhile, painted a logo on his little white Jabiru, "Pauline Hanson One Nation Fed Up Tour," and flew his leader to the Mount Isa Rotary Rodeo and the Birdsville Races, to Yeppoon and Great Keppel Island, and to a Reclaim Australia rally in Rockhampton. Hanson explained:

> As I have travelled around the country, people are telling me they are fed up with losing the farming sector, they're fed up with foreign ownership of our land and prime agricultural land, they're fed up with the threat of terrorism in our country and the free trade agreements that have been signed, which are not in our best interest, and foreign workers coming in to Australia … so hence the "Fed Up" tour.

She was recruiting candidates for the election Turnbull might call at any moment. Before flying north she appealed "for people who are like-minded to Pauline, and the party's beliefs, to show their interest in standing for Parliament." Candidates were a perennial problem. Over the years she had endorsed various debtors and bankrupts; a professional Santa; a truck driver with prior convictions; a guy who thought Pope John Paul sold cyanide gas to the Nazis; a car detailer who roughed up his customers; a policewoman who called the Indigenous "oxygen thieves" with a "disgusting aversion to work"; and a young woman who thought Islam was a country. Hanson said: "She's not ready."

In late February last year James Ashby woke to find a furious email from One Nation's national treasurer, Ian Nelson. Trouble between them had been brewing for some time as Ashby moved to take further control of the party. Nelson, a Hanson fan who had held the faith through the hard years, bitterly resented the rise of the young man he called "the anti-Christ of politicians." According to Nelson, his early morning email read:

> Need to talk, sport … Don't you ever speak to anyone about a possible candidate for this party unless you discuss it with the executive … Do not meet with anyone unless you clear it with me first. You have been in this party for a very short time. Respect our constitution and rules of process … share with the executive … no secrets please, not in this party.

The party was heading for another purge. Oldfield had conducted the first when he ousted Pasquarelli. Another came when Oldfield departed. A third claimed Hanson herself all those years ago. Now she was back with a new man at her side – a man she would soon be calling "my adopted son" – and her old retainers were fractious. It's a story that goes a long way back: courtiers feuding for the ear of their ruler. The flashpoint of the dispute was the choice of candidates. Yet whatever transpired between Ashby and Nelson in the aftermath of that angry email did nothing to improve the quality of the men and women being endorsed by One Nation. They were a rag-tag bunch of dreamers, conspiracy theorists and serial candidates who saw in Pauline Hanson the best hope they had ever had of realising their dreams. Once chosen they were directed to order their "starter pack" of corflutes, business cards and flyers from Ashby's firm Coastal Signs & Printing. Price: $3500.

Elise Chapman was chosen to head the One Nation Senate ticket in Victoria. The Bendigo City councillor had made her name provoking a huge ruckus to stop a mosque being built in the town. When news broke of her place on the One Nation ticket, she told the *Australian*: "I think we only have to learn from France and Sweden and Norway and the rape capital of the world now, Germany. I think Merkel has just wrecked Germany. I just think our country's at a real turning point now." Hanson launched Chapman's campaign at the mighty Shamrock Hotel. In answer to a pro-mosque tweet a few weeks later, Chapman posted a graphic image of female genital mutilation. Locals were appalled. Petitions were signed. She withdrew from the election for "personal reasons." Hanson wished her the best.

Peter Rogers, a Cairns businessman, was endorsed for the Cape York seat of Leichhardt. His fixations were par for the course for One Nation – halal certification, UN plans for global dominance, the hoax of global warming – but then he posted on his website the claim that Aylan Kurdi, the three-year-old washed up on a Turkish beach in late 2015, was in fact alive and well. Rogers listed the fake dead toddler with other deceptions that changed the world. "The greatest social changes that happen in Australia are founded on total lies and a fabricated incident. Look at Port Arthur." He stood for the party in 2016, but after that post in early 2017 One Nation cut him loose.

Malcolm Roberts, diminutive former mining engineer and leader of the climate-denying Galileo Movement (patron: Alan Jones), was endorsed for the Senate ticket in Queensland. Hanson had turned to Roberts for advice during the Lockyer campaign. Roberts told the Monthly that she asked: "Tell me about this carbon dioxide thing, and climate change being caused by humans." When he told her it was all a sham, she said: "I guessed that." But what lay behind the sham? According to Roberts, a cabal of Jewish banking families was working behind the facades of the UN, the US Federal Reserve and the Bank of England to install a worldwide socialist government. Roberts has also toyed at times with the sovereign citizen movement, which reckons governments are corporations in disguise whose clutches can be evaded by clever use of punctuation. Hence his 2011 affidavit to Julia Gillard:

> I, Malcolm-Ieuan: Roberts., the living soul has not seen or been presented with any material facts or evidence that the Commonwealth of Australia CIK#000805157 is not a corporation registered on the United States of America securities exchange ...

He and Hanson talked for twelve hours face to face before she offered him a place on the ticket. Only then did he begin to read up on Islam. He didn't like what he learnt: "It is an ideology of hate."

The Big Kahuna: Rod Culleton was billed as a rural action militant helping farmers fighting off predatory banks. What might have been Culleton's one moment of fame came on 60 Minutes, but Hanson took a shine to the rugged battler. Attempts were made to warn her about the other side of the man: a number of unhappy former business associates were pursuing him. He had been bankrupt. Charges were pending. Bruce Bell, one of the pursuers, sent a dossier on Culleton to One Nation. Angry treasurer Ian Nelson would later tell the Australian he didn't pass the material on to Hanson: "Why the hell would I? It had nothing to do with them. I knew they were plotting to get rid of Rod, and you know the rules. Keep your enemy close ... I wanted to know what Bell had."

As Hanson was gathering her team, Malcolm Turnbull handed her two gifts. First, the rules for electing senators were changed so that voters — rather than backroom strategists — decided where their preferences went. The aim was to put Glenn Druery out of business but the change meant the vote-whisperer could no longer muster little parties to block Hanson. She welcomed the reform: "Voters are in control of their votes this time.

I don't believe I'm going to be cheated out of a seat this time in where they direct their preferences." A week after a battle in the Senate delivered these voting reforms, Turnbull gave Hanson a second and more valuable gift: a double-dissolution election. It was a fateful call: a double dissolution would offer a useful way of attacking Labor for harbouring renegade building unions, but it would almost certainly see Pauline Hanson returned to Canberra. Turnbull weighed up the alternatives and opened the door to One Nation.

The date was set for 2 July. Evidence is hard to find that One Nation's campaign was driven by economic imperatives. True, the platform attacked free trade as passionately as ever, but offered nothing much more than angry demands that it should end. Twenty years down the track Hanson was still pushing the party's old agenda of eccentric taxes and cheap money for farmers. The second dot point on the Economics and Tax Policy was freshly harvested from the cosmos of deep conspiracy:

> Restore Australia's constitution so that our economy is run for the
> benefit of Australians instead of the United Nations and unaccount-
> able foreign bodies that have interfered and have choked our econ-
> omy since the federal government handed power to the International
> Monetary Fund in 1944.

Hanson also had little to say about education or health. She renewed her old attacks on the divorce courts. She endorsed an equal marriage plebiscite. She promised to pursue welfare cheats and "uncover the disgraceful entitle-ments given to all politicians." Gun laws would be relaxed. She hammered foreign ownership, particularly of power plants and farmland.

But her real energies were spent gathering the race vote. She cam-paigned against building mosques and wearing burqas. She called for all Muslim immigration and all refugee programs to end. She demanded a royal commission to investigate the true nature of Islam: religion or ideo-logy of hate? The slaughter by Omar Mateen of fifty people in a gay nightclub in Florida came in the midst of all this and Hanson seized the moment, posting a grim warning that an Australian Orlando was just down the road:

> We have laws here that we don't bring in pitbull terriers because they are a danger to our security. We don't bring in certain toys because they are a danger to our society and to our children … so … pressure the government to say no more Muslims in Australia. No more Muslim refugees in Australia. Take a strong stance. Protect our security, our safety on our streets and our people.

That spray was one of her big Facebook hits of the campaign. Nothing she said in those weeks about employment, manufacturing, free trade or globalisation had remotely that impact. All but one of her big hits dealt with race:

> 23 February:
> "Why is it we constantly hear the Australian Government wants to cut Australia's aged pension scheme, YET foreign aid, politicians entitlements and economic refugees have an open cheque book?"
> 13,000 likes

> 8 March:
> "You don't have to be White to be Australian. We only ask you learn to read and write English, respect our flag, abide by our laws and constitution and join in with the rest of us."
> 14,000 likes

> 13 June:
> Orlando: "We have laws here that we don't bring in pitbull terriers …"
> 15,000 likes

> 16 June, after the Iftar dinner:
> "I'm not quite lost for words, but close to it after Malcolm Turnbull hosted a special 'appeasers' dinner at Kirribilli House last night."
> 14,000 likes

21 June:

"Sharia banking in the budget"

      17,000 likes

The Australian Election Study showed the race message was resonating with a significant cohort of Hanson's voters after her posts. The AES asked: "During the 2016 election campaign did you access the official party or candidate campaign sites?" Yes:

National	13 per cent
Liberal	14 per cent
Labor	20 per cent
One Nation	34 per cent
Green	40 per cent

Ian McAllister says the AES shows newspapers and television losing their sway and an exponential rise in the importance of the internet during the last three or four elections. But not for all voters and all parties: "What those figures for One Nation reflect is that minor parties find social media is an incredibly efficient and low-cost way of micro-targeting voters."

Hanson had already taken on the lustre of a winner. The only question was: how many people would she bring over the line with her on polling day? Old party disciplines broke down. Voters took advantage of the simpler Senate paper to send preferences her way as never before. The result was terrible for the Coalition. Labor picked up two seats in Queensland, Herbert and Longman, both on the strength of One Nation preferences. Hanson sailed into the Senate with 9.2 per cent of the Queensland vote and brought Malcolm Roberts with her. Had she won 150 more votes in Tasmania she would have led a squad of five senators to Canberra. Four was remarkable enough: two Queenslanders, plus Brian Burston in New South Wales and Culleton in Western Australia. The One Nation block would be the biggest after the Greens. She would have what she did not have twenty years earlier: leverage. Polling analyst Tim Colebatch wrote:

"No rebel party on the right has achieved that since the DLP was at its peak half a century ago." Her return reignited interest in her.

By the time she rose to make her second maiden speech last September, opinion polls showed her national following was at 6 per cent and rising. The Senate was crowded. For the occasion she wore a teal blue suit and a look of resigned triumph:

> It has taken numerous elections, countless legal battles and doing a stint in maximum security on trumped-up charges – of which former speaker Bronwyn Bishop stated I was Australia's first political prisoner – to find myself here. Some call it persistence and tenacity. My daughter describes it as a Johnny Farnham comeback. I call it standing up and fighting for what you believe in and not allowing the bastards to grind you down. So, to all my peers in this place and those from the past, I have two words for you: I'm back – but not alone.

It was not like the last time. She had to be wooed. Her votes were the surest path through the Senate for government legislation. Her old enemies were all over her. She spent hours with the prime minister. She had his number and he always took her calls. She made up with Tony Abbott, the man who helped send her to prison. Michaelia Cash was the government's go-to girl for getting Hanson's attention. And it wasn't hard to get: Hanson is still at heart the savvy owner of a little business who joined the party in Ipswich and won pre-selection in 1995 because they thought she was "a classic Liberal." She walked her team over to the government benches to support spending and welfare cuts. When the time came, she backed penalty-rate cuts. On the question of business: One Nation was given $1,745,369 public funding after its 2016 success. That brings to roughly $7,000,000 what she and her party have been paid since she first hit the political trail. Fresh spoils of office in 2017 – a staff in Canberra – brought to a head the tensions building inside the party since James Ashby appeared on the scene. The old guard in Queensland walked. Staff were fired, denouncing her and her *consigliere*. At this time, the Commonwealth Director of Public Prosecutions decided to lay no charges over Ashby's role in leaking the Slipper diaries.

Office favours Hanson. Once back on the map she effortlessly provoked publicity. Her return was a big story. This time, *60 Minutes* was kind. Her plans for One Nation engaged voters across Australia. Her national support grew steadily from not much more than 4 to over 9 per cent, where it still stands. That puts about 1,500,000 voters in play. In Queensland her support swiftly doubled to 23 per cent, the same following that won her party eleven seats all those years ago. The political establishment trembled. But the notion that she was leading an immensely powerful populist uprising was always overblown. So too the continual comparisons drawn between her and Donald Trump. Her backers and his share something of the same background and the same views. But Hanson never had the numbers.

Turnbull ran another do-nothing government, with Hanson as the new excuse for nothing being done. Her followers must not be antagonised, it was said, by pushing for changes this country has wanted for a long time. Conservative governments in the United Kingdom and New Zealand have made equal marriage law and taken useful measures to combat climate change. But not here, not even after a decade or more of political brawling. Logjam continues to be the natural order of Australian politics. Though Hanson is widely regarded as the voice of those whose wages have been falling behind, the Turnbull government has come up with nothing much to address the problem. That's perhaps more than we can expect of the Coalition. At least Turnbull didn't go about praising – in the face of Hanson's anti-Muslim diatribes – the wonders of free speech. But he followed in Howard's footsteps, not contesting her on race. As prime minister, he sent two messages: one to the bush and another to the cities.

George Christensen, the National member for the sugar coast who celebrated his recent conversion to the Antiochian Orthodox Church with a tattoo of the Virgin Mary, spoke to the bush. He blasted Muslims and begged One Nation not to stand against him in Dawson. Weeks later, Russell Broadbent, the voice of the city, rose to deplore Christensen's words:

> It is time for us to rise above the politics of fear and division, because our love of diversity, difference and freedom will endure. Our love of the rule of law, of respect for one another and of tolerance of each other will endure. Our love of freedom of religion, of freedom of speech and of country will endure. Our love of shared values, of a fair go for all and of shared responsibilities will endure.

Though widely acclaimed, Broadbent's appeal for calm and decency went unheeded in his own party. No Liberal MP backed him. Within days, the Minister for Immigration, Peter Dutton, was on his feet attacking Malcolm Fraser for letting Muslim Lebanese into the country forty years ago. The reason? "Out of the last thirty-three people who have been charged with terrorist-related offences in this country, twenty-two are from second- and third-generation Lebanese Muslim backgrounds." Hanson couldn't have done the job better. Dutton's seat is, like Christensen's, under threat. His speech was condemned as widely as Broadbent's was applauded. But the day after its delivery he entered the Coalition party room to a great roar of approval. "Peter Dutton," Turnbull said, "is doing an outstanding job as immigration minister."

Bill Shorten can speak Hanson's lingo. Channelling the AWU official he once was, he talks sympathetically about giving industry a hand, making governments buy local, setting up a royal commission into the banks and cracking down on 457 visas. Though Shorten is willing to take Labor some way into One Nation territory, he is holding the line on the progressive issues his opponents can't handle: renewable energy and equal marriage. He has no plans to tinker with the *Racial Discrimination Act*. But the leader of the Opposition is, like Turnbull, all but silent on the things that set One Nation apart: immigration and race. He has delegated to Penny Wong the task of attacking Hanson as a racist. He doesn't do that sort of thing himself. Labor needs Hanson's Senate votes as much as the government does. She is the gatekeeper of legislation for at least a couple of years yet. Even so, Labor won't be doing preference deals with her. Shorten said: "You've got to stand for something in politics."

The deal in Western Australia was an exercise in many things: in forgetting, in desperation, in what makes Australians despise politicians. Here was a government doing what governments seem to spend all their time doing: manoeuvring for survival. That this meant the Liberals endorsing a race-baiting protectionist didn't matter. Their primary vote had fallen to 29 per cent, so anything was worth a go. Yet the campaign held two lessons that we shouldn't forget in a hurry. The first is the power of the right question. Hanson had a terrible last week of the campaign because Barrie Cassidy asked her about her hostility to the vaccination of children. He asked her about many things on *Insiders* that morning — what she thought of Muslims and Vladimir Putin and penalty rates – but this was the one that did the damage. It dogged her because it showed her in plain light to be a crackpot. And the second, more important than the first, is that the far right where politicians are spending so much energy harvesting votes these days is not Australia. Nearly all of us are somewhere else, scattered around the centre, waiting for a government that will take this good, prosperous, generous country into the future.

SOURCES

I hope this essay puts a floor of fact under speculation about Hanson's people and her political appeal. Thus, I cannot sufficiently thank Andrew Markus of the Scanlon Foundation and Ian McAllister of the Australian Election Study, who dug into their research for me and patiently helped me come to grips with the numbers. Murray Goot of Macquarie University was again – as he has been often in the last twenty years – my tutor in polling on race in Australian politics. Great help was given to me by Rebecca Huntley; Antony Green; the splendid Katharine Murphy; George Megalogenis; the filmmaker Anna Broinowski; political party researchers who, alas, must remain anonymous; and an army of colleagues whose work over the last twenty years I acknowledge in the text and these endnotes. Two researchers shaped the essay profoundly: Henry Sherrell, Research Officer at the Australian National University, and Dom Kelly, political commentator, doctoral candidate and one of the extended Black Inc. family. I have been saved too often to count by the sharp eyes of Kirstie Innes-Will. My editor, Chris Feik, is a phenomenon. I've no idea where he gets his patience.

Pauline Hanson never got back to me.

1	"Hi, everyone": Video posted to Pauline Hanson's Please Explain Facebook page, 9 November 2016.
2	"She's got the art": Simon Hunt to me, 19 January 2017.
3	"I've just been told": Channel 7 News, 20 January 2017.
4	"It is not a single issue party": Australian, 13 February 2017.
4	"RACIST JIBES": Herald Sun, 4 March 1996.
4	"RACISM THE WORST": Australian Financial Review, 5 March 1996.
4	"RACISM IN POLITICS": Australian, 9 March 1996.
4	"RACISM THE UGLY EXPRESSION": Australian, 11 March 1996.
4	"HANSON STANDS": Daily Telegraph, 22 March 1996.
4	"a voice of responsibility": Tony Abbott, 2GB radio, 17 February 2017.
4–5	"Racist politics are evil": Australian, 22 June 1998.
5	"Politics is relentlessly driven": Sydney Morning Herald, 15 September 2015.
8	"Pauline Hanson's group": Jeff Kennett to me, 18 January 2017.
9	"Doing the deal": Guardian, 12 March 2017.
9	"If you're not prepared": 7.30, ABC TV, 15 February 2017.
10	"What I could see": All Peter Scanlon quotes to me, 22 February 2017.
11	"The latest survey": Andrew Markus, Mapping Social Cohesion: The Scanlon Foundation Surveys 2016, Scanlon Foundation with Monash University and the Australian Multicultural Foundation, 2016.

14   "Eighty-five per cent": Andrew Markus quotes are to me unless otherwise indicated.

14   "a world survey": Jacob Poushter, "Diversity Welcomed in Australia, U.S. Despite Uncertainty over Muslim Integration", Pew Research Center (online) 6 February 2017.

15   "emerging signs": *Mapping Social Cohesion 2016*, p. 4 and table 14.

15   "2016 report": Andrew Markus, *Australians Today: The Australia@2015 Scanlan Foundation Survey*, Scanlon Foundation with Monash University and the Australian Multicultural Foundation, 2016.

16   "Essential reported": Essential, "Ban on Muslim Migration", Essential Report (online), 21 September 2016, <www.essentialvision.com.au/ban-on-muslim-immigration>.

16   "In October": Roy Morgan Research, "Majority of Australians support Muslim & Asylum seeker immigration; and 58% want Australia's population kept under 35 million", Finding No. 7017, 25 October 2016.

19   "She wasn't given": *Sydney Morning Herald*, Good Weekend, 30 November 1996, p. 18.

19   "I lost my seat": Pauline Hanson, *Untamed & Unashamed: The Autobiography*, JoJo Publishing, 1 April 2007, pp. 63–4.

19   "The majority of politicians": *Untamed & Unashamed*, p. 61.

19–20 "She was a good bit": *Sydney Morning Herald*, Good Weekend, 30 November 1996.

20   "If you want anything": *Untamed & Unashamed*, p. 25.

21   "Fallu cannot convince": *Sydney Morning Herald*, 30 March 1996, p. 32.

21   "I loved political discussions": *Untamed & Unashamed*, p. 61.

21   "I had no documentation": *Untamed & Unashamed*, p. 7.

22   "Black deaths in custody": *Queensland Times*, 6 January 1996.

23   "calculated and callous attack": *Untamed & Unashamed*, p. 69.

23   "I will not back down": *Queensland Times*, 14 February 1996.

23   "It was like": *Sydney Morning Herald*, 21 August 2003.

23   "Missions were very much": John Howard to me, June 1998.

24   "stalled in his old attitudes": Alan Walker to me, June 1998.

24   "Howard showed no interest": Ian Viner to me, June 1998.

24   "On what grounds": "Aboriginal Land Rights: A View" in Australian Mining Industry Council, *Minerals Outlook Seminar Proceedings*, 1984, p. 88.

25   "I do not accept the view": *Age*, 23 November 1993.

25   "that it is impossible": Andrew Markus, *Race: John Howard and the Remaking of Australia*, Allen & Unwin, 2001, p. 87.

25   "special benefits": Ian McAllister and Anthony Mughan, *Australian Election Study 1987, Study Documentation*.

26   "We need ... to reduce": *Australian Financial Review*, 12 August 1988.

26   "slowed down": *Sydney Morning Herald*, 1 August 1988.

26   "territorial dismemberment": *Age*, 28 July 1993.

27   "Whatever the merits": David Barnett with Pru Goward, *John Howard: Prime Minister*, Viking, 1997, p. 718.

27   "There is a shadow": *Sydney Morning Herald*, 5 March 1996.

27   "de-wogging": *Australian*, 17 February 1996.

28   "little slanty-eyed": *Independent* 15 February 1996.

28   "We know there": *Sydney Morning Herald*, 4 March 1996.

28   "For while it": *Sydney Morning Herald*, 5 March 1996.

28   "a political masterpiece": *Race*, p. 155.

28–9 "tremors like an earthquake": *Untamed & Unashamed*, p. 92.

30   "You ought to be able": *Australian*, 27 February 2016.

31   "Out of cultural": *Australian*, 22 February 2017, p. 13.

31   "a law that strikes" and "It's time to change": *Australian*, 22 February 2017, p. 12.

31   "enemies of freedom": Senate, 13 February 2017.

31   "Asians": Maiden speech, House of Representatives, 10 September 1996.

32   "Now we are in danger": Second maiden speech, Senate, 14 September 2016.

32   "This nation is being divided" and "Abolishing the policy": Pauline Hanson, maiden speech, House of Representatives, 10 September 1996.

32   "People around the world": *Sky News*, 9 November 2016.

33   "Our common oppressors": *Pauline Hanson and George J. Merritt, Pauline Hanson – The Truth: On Asian Immigration, the Aboriginal Question, the Gun Debate and the Future of Australia,* Saint George Publishing, 1997, p. 155.

33   "My greatest desire" and "I am fed up": Maiden speech, House of Representatives, 10 September 1996.

34   "Indiscriminate immigration": Second maiden speech, Senate, 14 September 2016.

34   "unworkable socialist": House of Representatives, 4 March 1997

34   "Surely you have": Pauline Hanson's Please Explain Facebook page, 14 January 2017.

34   "If you're looking": Wayne Swan, Facebook post, 15 November 2016.

37   "John wanted a job": *Untamed & Unashamed*, p. 78.

37   "I came to learn": *Untamed & Unashamed*, p. 107.

37   "Even Jesus": *Sydney Morning Herald*, 17 June 1998.

38   "One of the great changes": John Howard, speech to Queensland Liberal State Council, 22 September 1996, quoted in Paul Kelly, *The March of Patriots: The Struggle for Modern Australia*, MUP, 2011, p. 368.

38   "Pauline Hanson was": John Howard, *Lazarus Rising: A Personal and Political Autobiography*, HarperCollins, 2010, p. 258.

38–9 "Could the impact": *Lazarus Rising*, p. 262.

39 "To my mind": *Lazarus Rising*, p. 258.

39 "Howard was smart": *Untamed & Unashamed*, p. 124.

39 "I don't": "Pauline 'Pantsdown'", <www.youtube.com/watch?v=8SxFc37h6js>.

40 "The Liberal Party generally": *Sydney Morning Herald*, 6 June 1998, p. 33.

41 "in two-party-preferred terms": *The March of Patriots*, p. 366.

42 "The major parties": Antony Green to me, 19 December 2016.

42 "In the House of Representatives": *Untamed & Unashamed*, p. 131.

43 "I don't have": Markus, *Race*, p. 189.

43 "We go out": *Daily Telegraph*, 15 February 2000.

44 "If I can invite": Maiden speech, House of Representatives, 10 September 1996.

44 "National security is": 2001 federal election campaign launch speech, 28 October 2001.

44–5 "In those days": Tim Colebatch, "Fear Puts One Nation Back Where It Counts", *Inside Story*, 4 August 2016, <http://insidestory.org.au/fear-puts-one-nation-back-where-it-counts>.

48 The Australian Election Study survey for 2016 was derived from a sample of 2818 completed returns. This was a raw response rate of 28.4 per cent from 12,497 questionnaires, adjusted to 29.9 per cent after accounting for those falling out of scope. The results presented here are weighted to reflect the characteristics of the electorate. The One Nation sample is proportional to the overall vote share in the 2016 election however this results in a small sample of One Nation voters for the AES. The adjusted sample was forty One Nation votes in the House of Representatives and seventy-three votes in the Senate, combining for a total of eighty individual responses who voted One Nation being sampled in the AES. The House of Representatives sample was used for the cross-party comparisons in "Pauline's People", while a combined sample was used for comparing the One Nation vote in 1998 and 2016. As Ian McAllister established, this sample is small for the purposes of empirical research. Therefore the AES is used to illustrate trends and differences instead of identifying precision in voter response. For more detail about the AES, please see pages 4 to 6 in *Australian Election Study, 2016: Study Documentation*, <http://australianelectionstudy.org>.

48 "We ask how people" and so on: Ian MacAllister to me, in several exchanges from December 2016 to February 2017.

49 "They get themselves pregnant": *Australian*, 23 February 2017.

49–50 "We're a little shielded": Rebecca Huntley to me, January 2017.

51 "educational inequality": Matthew Goodwin and Oliver Heath, "Brexit Vote Explained: Poverty, Low Skills and Lack of Opportunities", Joseph Rowntree

Foundation (online), 31 August 2016, <www.jrf.org.uk/report/brexit-vote-explained-poverty-low-skills-and-lack-opportunities>.

51   "the education gap": Nate Silver, "Education, Not Income, Predicted Who Would Vote for Trump", FiveThirtyEight (online), 22 November 2016, <http://fivethirtyeight.com/features/education-not-income-predicted-who-would-vote-for-trump/>.

53   "If they think": Kosmos Samaras to me, 13 December 2016.

61   "If you say": Samaras to me.

62   "I threw my hands" and "I wasn't going": *Untamed & Unashamed*, pp. 204 & 205.

62   "The system let me down": *Courier-Mail*, 8 November 2003, p. 33.

63   "So there was never": *Sydney Morning Herald*, News Review, 30 August 2003, p. 30.

63   "How else": *Sydney Morning Herald*, Spectrum, 11 March 2000, p. 1.

64   "Mr Ettridge and Mr Oldfield", "We are not", "When Mr Archer" and "Those members of": *Sharples v O'Shea & Anor* [1999] QSC 190, pars 105, 107, 119 & 132.

65   "I felt the cold, heavy handcuffs": *Untamed & Unashamed*, p. 13.

65   "You have to realise": *Daily Telegraph*, 20 February 2003, p. 7.

65   "the final fizz": *Daily Telegraph*, 28 March 2003, p. 29.

65   "inexperienced trial counsel" and "and because": *R v. Hanson; R v Ettridge* [2003] QCA 488, pars 40 & 28.

65   "I want": *Enough Rope with Andrew Denton*, ABC, 20 September 2004.

66   "She said she stood": *Age*, 16 September 2004, p. 10.

67   "about a third of the nation": Sarah M. Cameron and Ian McAllister, Australian Election Study, *Trends in Australian Public Opinion 1987–2016*, Canberra: ANU, 2016, "Attitudes towards policies on Indigenous Australians" graph, p. 96.

67–8 "Young boys were" and "cast aside the": *Untamed & Unashamed*, p. 271.

67–8 "Our governments have bent" and "We're bringing in": AAP, "Hanson Turns on 'Diseased' Africans", *Sydney Morning Herald*, 6 December 2006.

68   "I haven't put all this": *Sunday Mail*, 27 April 2008.

69   "Would you consider": *Australian*, 2 March 2009, p. 6.

69   "The young woman's nasal bridge": *Sydney Morning Herald*, 18 March 2009.

69   "It's overrun": *Daily Telegraph*, 14 November 2010.

69   "Australia needs me": *Herald Sun*, 10 March 2011.

69   "I think the government": *Sydney Morning Herald*, 13 April 2011, p. 5.

70   "public service": *Sydney Morning Herald*, 5 November 2016.

70   "The One Nation founder's Senate bid": *Canberra Times*, 17 June 2013.

70   "one or two parties that are frankly racist": *Sydney Morning Herald*, 21 August 2013.

71   "Yes, they have" and "Women in hijabs": *Sydney Morning Herald*, Good Weekend, 13 July 2013, p. 20.

72   "Don't get me": *Sunday Mail*, 10 January 2015.

72   "He is untrustworthy" and "Pauline's comments": *Australian*, 14 January 2015, p. 4.

72   "just a one-day thing": *Courier-Mail*, 1 February 2015, p. 9.

72   "A person who" and "I challenge": *Enough Rope with Andrew Denton*, ABC, 20 September 2004.

75   "I do not accept": *Sydney Morning Herald*, 13 December 2005.

75   "Love Nulla" and "They cover up": *GQ Australia*, 1 December 2015.

75   "Islam is proving": Pauline Hanson's One Nation Islam Policy, <www.onenation.com.au/policies/islam>.

75   "To claim that Islam": Philip Dorling, *The American Far-Right Origins of Pauline Hanson's Views on Islam*, The Australia Institute, p. 11.

75   "How could they square": Dorling, *The American Far-Right Origins of Pauline Hanson's Views on Islam*, p. 12.

76   "is singing from": Dorling, *The American Far-Right Origins of Pauline Hanson's Views on Islam*, p. 23.

76–8   "She literally": Anne Aly to me, February 2017.

79   "What annoys me": *Enough Rope with Andrew Denton*, ABC, 20 September 2004.

80   "She's won many positions": *Herald Sun*, 15 April 2009.

81   "When it comes to": Abbott, 5 August 2014.

81   "As far as the Daesh death cult": Tony Abbott, AAP, 27 June 2015.

81   "I've often heard": Abbott, 23 February 2015.

81   "The Nazis did": Abbott, 3 September 2015.

81   "promoting hatred": *Guardian*, 23 February 2015.

82   "A vote for me": Pauline Hanson's Please Explain Facebook page, 6 October 2015.

82   "People of Australia": News.com.au, 6 July 2016.

82   "RELIGION OF 'PEACE'": Pauline Hanson's Please Explain Facebook page, 14 November 2015.

82–3   "Muslims were seen" and "Do you honestly want": Reclaim Australia speech, 19 April 2015.

83   "The installation of Malcolm": Rebecca Huntley, *Still Lucky: Why You Should Feel Optimistic about Australia and Its People*, Viking, 2017, p. 55–6.

83   "They are Liberal members": *Australian*, 26 September 2015.

84   "I am only": *Australian*, 18 July 2015.

84   "Did you ask": *60 Minutes*, Channel 9, 29 November 2015.

84–5   "As I have" and "for people who": "Hanson Kicks off Her 'Fed Up' Tour Tomorrow", Pauline Hanson's One Nation website, 16 July 2015.

85   "oxygen thieves": *Sunday Mail* (Queensland), 10 January 2015.

85 "She's not ready": Daniel Piotrowski and AAP, "One Nation's Stephanie Banister Withdraws from Election Campaign", 10 August 2013.

85 "the anti-Christ" and "Need to talk, sport": *Australian*, 7 January 2017.

85 "my adopted son": *Sydney Morning Herald*, 21 January 2017.

86 "I think we only have to learn": *Australian*, 9 January 2016.

86 "The greatest social": "The Drowned Boy, the Lie That Changed the World", <https://web.archive.org/web/20170112120324/http:/peterrogersonenation.com/the-drowned-boy-the-lie-that-changed-the-world/>.

86 "Tell me about": *Monthly*, November 2016, p. 12.

87 "I, Malcolm-Ieuan: Roberts.,": *Sydney Morning Herald*, 6 August 2016.

87 "It is an ideology of hate": *Weekend Australian Magazine*, 22–23 October 2016.

87 "Why the hell would I?": *Australian*, 7 January 2017.

87–8 "Voters are in control": *Saturday Paper*, 23 April 2016.

88 "Restore Australia's constitution": "Economics & Tax Policy", Pauline Hanson's One Nation website, <www.onenation.com.au/policies/economics/economics-2?>.

88 "uncover the disgraceful": One Nation policies flyer, <www.onenation.com.au/LiteratureRetrieve.aspx?ID=155063>.

89 "We have laws": Video posted to Pauline Hanson's Please Explain Facebook page, 13 June 2016.

89 "Why is it": Pauline Hanson's Please Explain Facebook page, 23 February 2016.

89 "You don't have": Pauline Hanson's Please Explain Facebook page, 8 March 2016.

89 "We have laws": Video posted to Pauline Hanson's Please Explain Facebook page, 13 June 2016.

81 "I'm not quite": Pauline Hanson's Please Explain Facebook page, 16 June 2016.

90 "Sharia banking": Pauline Hanson's Please Explain Facebook page, 21 June 2016.

90 "What those figures": McAllister to me.

91 "No rebel party": Tim Colebatch, "Fear Puts One Nation Back Where It Counts", *Inside Story*, 4 August 2016, <http://insidestory.org.au/fear-puts-one-nation-back-where-it-counts>.

91 "It has taken": Second maiden speech, Senate, 14 September 2016.

93 "It is time": House of Representatives, 7 November 2016.

94 "Out of the last": House of Representatives, 22 November 2016.

94 "Peter Dutton": *Sydney Morning Herald*, 23 November 2016.

94 "You've got to": *Guardian*, 2 February 2017.

THE AUSTRALIAN DREAM

Correspondence

Jacinta Nampijinpa Price

Stan's welcome comments as he begins his speech with greetings to his "Gadigal brothers and sisters" indicate the level of change that has taken place for a lot of Indigenous Australians "down south," as we say up here in the north. This greeting and the custom of addressing older people respectfully as "Aunty" or "Uncle" is a radical simplification of a complex kinship system. Warlpiri address each other by an exact kin term. We are all related in a particular way; we are not all just brothers and sisters. We do not use the terms "Aunty" and "Uncle" for anyone other than those who are in fact our aunty or uncle.

A re-creation and reinvention of culture is occurring down south; up here, in the Northern Territory and remote parts of Western Australia and South Australia where Indigenous languages are still spoken, we are different – not better, but different. Among those of us who identify as Indigenous in this country there is tremendous variation. At last Stan Grant is acknowledging this variety. I disagree with some of the points he makes in his Quarterly Essay, while respecting his right to think differently.

The media go looking for an "Aboriginal viewpoint," talk to some radical from a city with absolutely no knowledge of, or interest in, my part of the world, and then present that opinion as authentic, and somehow generalised. The media's acceptance of one view as "the Aboriginal view" is a bit like "They all look the same to me," only now it's "They all think the same as me." Yes, I call it a racist attitude.

I wasn't outraged by Bill Leak's cartoon. It was not a presentation of a racist stereotype. It was pointing out that there are some Aboriginal fathers who don't care about and do nothing for their kids. I know a few just like that. And I know a few white ones like that as well. I know some extremely decent and devoted Aboriginal fathers who were not the least bit worried by the cartoon, because they could see that he wasn't saying anything about them. We are capable of critical thinking.

My opinion of the Adam Goodes booing incident differs from Stan's as well. He rightly says that he does not know what was going on in the hearts of those who did the booing. He then decides to interpret it as an act of deeply offensive and hurtful racism. I have another interpretation. I believe many were reacting to the treatment meted out to the thirteen-year-old child for calling Goodes an ape. I don't associate the word "ape" with "Aboriginal," and I don't see why there should be an automatic connection. I have no doubt there were a few, not very bright, meat-headed racists among those booing. I have been taught not to be afraid of them and not to be hurt by them, but rather to pity them as the fools they are.

I have played sport all my life in Alice Springs. I now umpire men's Aussie Rules games and captain a women's team. My mother also played team sport in this town for around thirty years. In all that time, neither of us has been racially abused by whitefellas. The racists here are cowardly – outnumbered and out-gunned. However, both of us have been obscenely abused by drunken Aboriginal thugs in racist and misogynist terms. We are not hurt by them and we aren't afraid of them. We know they are pathetic, lost souls to be pitied, not feared.

Since I was a young teenager I have seen white friends racially abused and physically assaulted for being white by these same thugs. I have often acted as a bodyguard for them. As an umpire, I have had to admonish Aboriginal spectators at football games for calling Aboriginal players "f—g whitefella lovers" because they are happy to play in racially mixed teams. What is more hurtful: being called an "ape" by a thirteen-year-old girl, or being abused by your own mob because you have no problem counting whitefellas among your friends and teammates? White sportspeople put up with continual racial abuse because they feel that the *Racial Discrimination Act* doesn't apply to them and because they have enough Aboriginal friends and supporters to know that their abusers, just like white racists, are a small, ignorant, mentally unstable minority.

I am happy that Stan Grant tells us of the large number of Aboriginal Austral-ians who have taken what is on offer and, building on the strength and dignity of their ancestors, have made a good life for themselves and their families. I, too, know of the sad history. In 1928, when my grandfather was in his mid-teens, he was hunting in the bush around 35 kilometres south of George Murray's police party while they were shooting probably over 100 innocent people in reprisal for the death of one white man. My grandfather also told a local historian of a massacre of perhaps ten to fifteen men, women and children by white pastoral-ists in response to the killing of a draft horse.

Yes, I know the stories. I also know that not all the killers were white. I have also been told of the murder of my people by black killers. I know that my Irish great-great-great-grandfather was not given a choice when he was sent to this country in chains in his mid-twenties in 1833. He and his descendants didn't kill anybody. I know that my white father's family accepted my Aboriginal mother with loving enthusiasm and that my Warlpiri family did the same for my father. There is no racism in our families. My grandparents, white and black, taught me that race doesn't matter.

I would now like to see people like Stan Grant, those who have made the big time, add to their story of victimhood and oppression a story of determination, personal responsibility, hope and success. I would like to see those who have made it reach out their hands in a practical way to help those who are trying to keep their languages and traditions intact and cope with the contemporary world. Teach them not to become useless, stereotypical victims. I want my people to succeed and I want their children saved from an early grave because of violence, sexual abuse, substance abuse and despair, all within their own families and communities. Like Kevin Gilbert said years ago – "because a white man'll never do it."

Jacinta Nampijinpa Price

Amy McQuire

Stan Grant says he does not want to seem "immodest" when he mentions his long career as a reporter — a career that has spanned three decades and some of the greatest events of our time. He goes on to give part of the credit for his success to the fact he did not seek the Indigenous round as a young, up-and-coming journalist. Thus, he was not "marginalised" by it, he writes in his Quarterly Essay.

Grant says the ABC "has been recruiting and training Indigenous people "for decades," but it is "still to produce a single Indigenous foreign correspondent, Four Corners reporter or host of a prime-time national program." He finishes: "I suspect, though, that is about to change." If there is one thing Grant got right in his essay, it was that. This year he began fronting the summer edition of 7.30.

In his essay, Grant looks at his own privilege and that of the black "middle class," and asks: "The Australian Dream works for most of us; isn't it time to ask if it can work for all of us?" But Grant's version of the Australian Dream is a world away from the aspirations of many Aboriginal people. It is a dream fixated on the individual and "agency" — if by "agency" we mean choices that are about economic development.

This is a very limited view of black success, and that is probably because it is tied so heavily to Grant's own journey and identity.

According to Grant, the diplomacy for which some people, including me, have criticised him is a "reflection of the life I have made – the life my parents and grandparents prepared for me. I have moved from the fringes to the centre. I don't want to live in a country fractured by its history. I want to share in a sense of the possibilities of our nation. But nor do I want to live in a country that shrouds its past in silence."

But Grant has a different view of history to many other mob, some of whom he claims cling to this past to foster an identity of victimhood. He says memory and history "can embolden a sense of victimhood, a superiority of suffering.

History, suffering and culture can each encourage a narrowly conceived, 'essentialist' identity." But to remember the history of dispossession is not to make suffering and victimhood an integral part of Aboriginal identity. It is to acknowledge what came before – the phenomenal cultures and knowledge that existed on this continent long before the arrival of the British – and still survives today. This remembering is essential to Aboriginal identity.

We acknowledge the past, and call for others to remember it, because we understand how it seeps into the present. We see how successive governments have built up their own privileges on the backs of Aboriginal people, entrenching black disadvantage rather than eliminating it.

We remember history because it is the foundation on which any solution will have to be built.

Grant's own solutions are enmeshed in the ideas of the "migration" of mob into the mainstream economy and getting "a seat at the table," a share of the prosperity that is a result of this dispossession. His essay reads as a more eloquent version of the common plea that we should "get over it and move on."

One of its most jarring aspects is the characterisation of Aboriginal people as "economic migrants." Grant does admit he feels uncomfortable with this. It is strange to describe Indigenous peoples as being migrants in their own land: our experience will always be fundamentally different to that of later arrivals. He claims that even in the days of the frontier, "Indigenous people started to connect with the colonial economy." But he ignores the fact that Aboriginal people were slaves or earned unequal wages, and that their lives were completely controlled – surely important aspects to mention.

To glide over the psychological impact of being treated as slaves after having your own land stolen from you, of being classified as "flora and fauna," and then being expected to "assimilate" into the mainstream economy, even though access to this economy is extremely limited, seems like an incredible oversight. We still feel the echoes of this past mistreatment in official government policy (such as the Community Development Programme).

Grant characterises historical and intergenerational trauma as a convenient excuse, but it is extremely *inconvenient* for many Aboriginal people. It is not a historical fact that we have the luxury of forgetting, but a reality many have to deal with every day.

Early childhood development expert Dr Jan Hammill says, "People have heard the words trauma and intergenerational trauma and it becomes hackneyed, [but] we need to put it into a biological context. There are actual physiological changes going on." Biological, psychological and physiological changes began within the first generation of the invasion and have continued until the present. They have a direct impact on Indigenous Australians' capacity to move towards the mainstream economy. That is not to be defeatist, but rather to acknowledge that we must talk about the genesis of this trauma to understand for whom the Australian Dream works, and those whom it works actively against.

These are the mob who are being locked up at higher and higher rates, who are dying before their time, who are struggling to feed their families. They are the mob who are most likely to face the institutionalised racism Grant feels he has been able to rise above through his own ingenuity. This is the institutionalised racism entrenched in our health, education and justice systems, which often acts as a barrier to the very limited kind of success he espouses.

There is no point having an emerging black middle class and an "elite" if we still have Aboriginal people struggling at the grassroots level. They are dealing with the consequences of policies that directly target them, policies we are supposed to accept in order to do our own ladder-climbing.

Grant singles out a young female activist who "rejects" whiteness, acting out an "anti-white superiority," and argues that such thinking is "foolish" and "can lead to divisiveness." He writes that such identity politics are dangerous and claims that there is something "performative" about trying to revive and live culture – by, for instance, speaking "Aboriginal English" or wearing "possum-skin coats." But in fact it is whiteness that is divisive and violent. Yet it undergirds Australian institutions and culture.

In his essay, Grant takes us through the disastrous impacts of whiteness on Aboriginal people throughout Australia's history. Non-Indigenous Australia branded us the "other"; white has consistently been seen as the norm to aspire to. "White" is the norm in popular culture, in language and in the national holidays Australia has chosen to celebrate. White Australia controls Aboriginal policy, and what "self-determination" we have is very limited, almost caricaturised. Frequently television and radio segments on racism have all-white panels.

Grant thinks discussing this is "divisive," but I don't know how we can not discuss it. We must try to overcome it, as in the example Grant offers – of the Aboriginal people who chose to pass as white in order to gain access to the mainstream economy – those who saw the potential of the "Australian Dream."

Deconstructing whiteness is not about refusing knowledge, as Grant claims. It is about re-centring Aboriginal aspirations, rather than kowtowing to the historically catastrophic white Australian "dream" for us.

Grant says, "There are those among us – black and white – who eschew economic development and social uplift as a new, disguised form of assimilation, preferring instead a story of failure and blame – as though culture and spirituality are antithetical to a modern globalised world. To their minds, success is not 'black.'"

This is simplistic. No one chooses "failure and blame" – but this is where Grant's view of what constitutes "success" directly collides with that of many others. Few Aboriginal people would deny the right of other mob to engage with the economy. We celebrate many of our mob who have achieved the heights of fame and fortune. They, including Grant, are seen as role models. But the perception of "assimilation" arises when it seems like they are selling out their own people for their personal benefit; selling out the collective to strengthen the individual. This is antithetical to Aboriginal ways of life.

We are already seeing that the modern globalised world is simply not sustainable. It has thrived off feeding the rich while starving the poor, catering to the individual at the expense of the collective. It is killing the earth while filling the pockets of a select few.

Australia has built its prosperity on the foundation of Aboriginal poverty, and white Australians are still profiting from the destruction of Aboriginal lands. In many areas of the country, big miners continue to get rich from digging up the land, with Aboriginal people reaping very little financial reward.

The mob standing up to this are against the neoliberalism that has infiltrated Aboriginal policy over the past decades. This is where I find examples of Aboriginal agency, Aboriginal success and strength, even if they don't fit the conservative, neoliberal version of the Australian Dream.

Grant does not talk about the collective nature of Aboriginal politics and community; his essay is largely concerned with the individual – and most notably with himself.

That's why he sees becoming the first Aboriginal presenter of an ABC prime-time show as "success," while I look instead to the many Aboriginal people who have spent a lifetime building up the underfunded but crucial black media space so that we all have a voice, rather than just a select few.

Amy McQuire

George Megalogenis

Here's a trick question on our national identity: how long after the arrival of the First Fleet did it take for the Australian population to become more white than black? Twenty, fifty or 100 years?

The answer can be all of the above, or none. It depends on the people and the settlement. And it depends on what is meant by the words "white" and "black."

Europeans achieved their first majority in Van Diemen's Land in the 1810s. But they did not do so on the continent until the late 1830s, once the boats began carrying more free migrants than convicts to the colonies. Even then, the European majority was restricted to the southeast. To the north and west, they were still outnumbered. Queensland remained predominantly Indigenous until the 1860s; Western Australia until the 1880s; and the Northern Territory until the 1950s.

This probably overstates the speed of the "white" ascendancy. I used a conservative estimate of the Indigenous population in 1788: 314,500. Others have put the figure at closer to a million. We don't really know the starting point for the comparison. Nor is there any way to measure the people in between, those born locally with both migrant and Indigenous heritage.

These missing pieces in our colonial demography came to mind as I read Stan Grant's powerful essay. As he points out, most Indigenous people today are descendants of immigrants: "By the post-war era, many people identifying as Aboriginal had mixed heritage: for me, Irish convict stock and a white grandmother of English/German background." This got me thinking: how many "white" Australians with convict or free settler ancestors have "black" branches in their families of which they are not aware? The number need not be that large to make the point of a shared history. And the number is almost certainly much larger than most people imagine.

For the first century of Australia's short European history, the "white" population was excessively male. Consider the NSW census of 1833. The total population was 60,794, of which 43 per cent were free men and women, 40 per cent were convicts, and 17 per cent were children under twelve. The children split almost 50/50 between boys and girls. But 67 per cent of the free adults and 89 per cent of the convicts were male. After almost half a century of "settlement," the gender gap remained as in the First Fleet: three males for every female.

It doesn't take much imagination to suppose that European males took local Indigenous women as sexual partners, whether by consent or rape. The alternative is to assume that the surplus "white" men took a vow of celibacy or took to one another, or that the secret history of "white" Australia was a culture of female control, with each woman having two or three blokes.

When Queensland separated from New South Wales in 1859, it did so as a free settlement, but the gender imbalance persisted. There is a telling passage on this score in the 1861 census. "As a general rule, it may be safely laid down that a great disproportion of the sexes is a great evil, particularly where the population is dense and collected in large masses," the registrar-general, F.O. Darvall, wrote. "It however admits of some question whether this assertion is not weakened, and the evils considerably modified, by the peculiarly isolated condition of most of the inhabitants of the country portion of this Colony." The evils to which he referred were those that had troubled every governor since Arthur Phillip: grog, violence and prostitution. Colonial authorities were on a perpetual mission to civilise the "white" male through the importation of single women. So why would the Queensland bush be seen as the exception to this problem, when European men outnumbered European women by around three to one, and Indigenous people were still the majority?

Stan's essay reminds us that the White Australia Policy sought to erase that shared history. The Initial Conference of Commonwealth and State Aboriginal Authorities in Canberra in 1937 drew a colour line between the "half-caste" and other Indigenous Australians. "The destiny of the natives of aboriginal origin, but not the full blood, lies in their ultimate absorption by the people of the Commonwealth and it is therefore recommended that all efforts be directed in to that end," the conference resolved.

Stan has dug out a remarkable quote to explain the official thinking. The "half-castes" were to be absorbed on the same terms as "the Greek and Italian migrants," through the economy. That suggestion, from M.T. McLean, the Chief Protector of Aboriginals for South Australia, was probably meant as a compliment to the southern Europeans. Yet in the first half of the twentieth century, the Greeks and Italians were not quite "white" enough for Australia. Their numbers were restricted by conservative governments, and the Labor Party hounded those who were allowed to come. In the final week of the 1929 election campaign, Prime Minister Stanley Bruce addressed 3000 rowdy voters at the Prahran Town Hall in Melbourne. "When Mr. Bruce rose to speak there were shouts of 'Importer of black-fellows' and 'The Dagoes' friend,'" according to a report in the Hobart Mercury. My people only became "white" when the Vietnamese came in the 1970s. But we did it on our terms, as Greek and Italian Australians. Our newly acquired whiteness wasn't burdened with the demand that we disown our parents. We became "white" at the same time that multiculturalism replaced assimilation in immigration policy.

This is a key point that is misunderstood by conservatives obsessed with empowering bigotry in the name of free speech. Multiculturalism didn't divide the country; it saved it from tribalism. Imagine the division today if the postwar migrants and their local-born children had been told by Whitlam, Fraser, Hawke and Keating that they would continue to be treated as second-class citizens unless they renounced their heritage; if the groups with the highest rates of home ownership, with the best results in the classroom, and who were dominating the professions and industry were told they weren't really Australian.

This is the paradox I kept returning to as I read Stan's essay. He traces the rise of an Indigenous middle class that echoes the journey of the migrant. Yet there has been no equivalent change in Indigenous policy. Assimilation remains the default setting. "Black" means disadvantage; "white" means privilege. If an Indigenous Australian enters the mainstream, the question of colour becomes an accusation. You can't call yourself "black" if you've made it in the "white" world. You certainly can't ask government to change policy, let alone surrender the levers of paternalism to allow Indigenous Australians to decide what's best for their communities.

Then again, if an Indigenous Australian makes the footballer's journey from outcast to elite, they have to remain a certain type of "black" – humble, exceptional. They have to stand out as individuals in a team sport, their talent unsullied by training or game plans. When they kick a goal, they can't raise a defiant fist to the stand to rally their supporters and humiliate the other side; that is the domain of the white warrior.

Adam Goodes was a victim of this double standard. He had every word he uttered, every step he took on the sporting field, censured. His accusers claimed the right to free speech, and insisted he was obliged to listen. The booing increased in 2014, after he became Australian of the Year, and he was hounded through his final season for the Sydney Swans in 2015. Goodes had won two Brownlow Medals and played in two premierships. But those achievements had raised no ire in the stands. Footy fans only took offence after he spoke.

When they booed, Stan heard "a howl of humiliation" aimed at his people. We've talked about this often, reversing the normal discussion that occurs between league and footy fans. Not which game is better (sorry, Stan, it's Aussie Rules) but which spectator base is the less tolerant – the supposedly redneck fans in league's northern states, or the supposedly cultured folk who watch footy in the southern states? In other words, why did this happen at a game of Aussie Rules, and not rugby league? The answer lies, in part, in our colonial demography.

Here's a dirty secret of the tolerant southern states: they have little shared history with Indigenous Australia. The free migrants of Victoria and South Australia overran the "black" population within a decade of arrival, whereas it took half a century in New South Wales and Queensland. While Indigenous blood was spilled across the continent, in the rugby league states it was also decidedly more mixed.

Political leadership also matters. Twenty seasons before they started booing Adam Goodes, another shy Indigenous Australian footballer spoke out against racism and was greeted as a hero. Why was Michael Long able to do so in 1995? I suspect Paul Keating had something to do with it. When Long demanded action from AFL officials after an opponent called him a "black c—," he did so in an era that offered the promise of reconciliation. Keating had given his Redfern address at the end of 1992, and parliament had passed the *Native Title Act* twelve months later. Between these two landmarks, another Indigenous footballer, Nicky Winmar, had already made his name. They booed Winmar in 1993, but he lifted his jumper and pointed to his chest to say, "I'm black and I'm proud." Keating praised Winmar; the prime minister could have avoided the topic, but then he would have been just another politician.

Goodes was caught in the moral vacuum of Tony Abbott's government. This prime minister said nothing when it counted, giving license to conservative commentators to tell Goodes that he had brought the booing on himself.

With hindsight, Keating, not Abbott, was the exception. Keating was the last prime minister with an uncomplicated view of racial politics. He saw no point in appeasing the fringe; on the contrary, he understood that if he looked the other way when someone played the race card, whether on his own turf of politics, or against someone like Long on the footy field, he would lose his authority and Australia would become a little less cohesive.

Racism did not die with multiculturalism. What changed under the governments of Whitlam, Fraser, Hawke and Keating was the way the outsiders viewed themselves. They were told they belonged.

In the twenty years since Keating lost office, politicians have tried to accommodate racism, not out of any shared belief, but out of electoral panic. Yet the proportion of voters that can be motivated by calls to restrict immigration or to deny basic rights to Indigenous people has never been that great. As a rough rule of thumb, it sits somewhere between the 9 per cent who voted "No" at the 1967 referendum to allow Aborigines to be counted as part of the national census and the 4 per cent who voted for Pauline Hanson's One Nation in the Senate in 2016.

What is striking about Hanson's second coming is the Australians who trouble her. Her beef with multiculturalism is no longer with the Asians. We are now in danger of being swamped by Muslims, she says. But she hasn't shifted her position on Indigenous Australians. She still thinks they are claiming special benefits not available to ordinary Australians. It is too easy, she says, to call yourself an Aboriginal. She wants a debate on what defines an Aboriginal.

What was shocking about those particular comments was the absence of a comeback from Malcolm Turnbull or Bill Shorten. Then again, Hanson was merely reinforcing the status quo – a "white" politician wanting the final word on what it means to be "black." But I can't help wondering how the Queensland senator would feel if she found an Aboriginal ancestor in her family tree.

George Megalogenis

THE AUSTRALIAN DREAM

Marcia Langton

Stan Grant might seem very familiar to us, even reassuring; because of his television roles, he seems to be a taken-for-granted part of our lives. But there is something else going on in his Quarterly Essay, *The Australian Dream*, that may go unnoticed. His voice is fresh and fearless. We haven't heard this since before the tide of race-hate that John Howard and Pauline Hanson exploited in the 1990s to set a course for their idea of the Australian dream in which white people had not been budged from their seats at the peak of the old racial hierarchy. Australians like to believe they are not racist, that Australia is a tolerant and successful multicultural nation. Whether Indigenous or not, we have become inured to the peculiar style of racism that most believe does not exist. It exists in the many micro-aggressions that express the Australian style of racism, summed up by Paul Keating: "I'm not racist, but ..." Stan calls out these micro-aggressions: "You will hear people say, 'But you've done well.' Yes, I have, and I'm proud of it, and why have I done well? ... 'But you have white blood in you.'"

Stan's method is a dialectical argument with his ancestors and present-day Australia, and he has a special qualification to prosecute this debate: he was a reporter for a decade in war zones "from Iraq to Afghanistan and Pakistan." Coming home gave him a jolt. I experienced this in the 1970s; I left Queensland during the early Bjelke-Petersen era and when I arrived home in 1975, very little had changed. The vicious daily racism directed at me was a shock that shaped my aspirations and career for a lifetime.

Stan wants to believe in the Australia that is extolled as the most successful multicultural nation, but his own family history — the racist and degrading treatment of his own forebears who withstood it all — gives the lie to this nationalist fantasy. He wants to say with other Australians, "We are better than this," but the treatment of AFL superstar Adam Goodes, booed off the field repeatedly by craven racists, cracks the image of Australia as "an extraordinary country ... the envy of the world."

His contest with the idea of the "Australian Dream" is a powerful reply to John Howard's "comfortable Australia" and Geoffrey Blainey's "black armband" dismissal of the toll that colonisation and nation-building took on Stan's people from the plains of New South Wales and the many other Aboriginal societies across the continent. Stan's eloquence is very welcome after two decades of bitter wrangling about the blatantly clear historical facts: "If I was sitting here where my friends are tonight, I would be arguing passionately for this country. But I stand here with my ancestors, and the view looks very different from where I stand." He reminds us of the grandeur of moments in our recent history, such as Cathy Freeman lighting the Olympic torch, but rebounds with this: "But every time we are lured into the light, we are mugged by the darkness of this country's history."

The debate between those who deny the history of people such as Stan's own parents and grandparents, and those who want a civil and tolerant society based on a courageous reckoning with the past, has subsided from the roar of Howard's era to a nasty whisper – on the good days. On the bad days, it is, as Stan says, "a howl." It is difficult for the victims of racism to find the words to describe the wounds of this special type of hatred, and here Stan has made his mark, like a James Baldwin for our times. Of the Adam Goodes episode, he says:

> Thousands of voices rose to hound an Indigenous man. A man who was told he wasn't Australian. A man who was told he wasn't Australian of the Year. And they hounded that man into submission.
>
> I can't speak for what lay in the hearts of the people who booed Adam Goodes. But I can tell you what we heard when we heard those boos. We heard a sound that was very familiar to us.
>
> We heard a howl. We heard a howl of humiliation that echoes across two centuries of dispossession, injustice, suffering and survival. We heard the howl of the Australian Dream, and it said to us again: you're not welcome.

These were just a few lines from his speech on 27 October 2015 at the City Recital Hall in Sydney. "Blood, history and becoming" is an apt subtitle for the remainder of this stinging essay. The Ethics Centre posted the video of this speech and it went viral. This surprised Stan, but his response is one that doesn't surprise me. Sharing the facts of our family histories with an audience such as listened to Stan at the Ethics Centre – telling the facts of the humiliation and brutalisation suffered by our parents and grandparents – is a doubling of the trauma. This is a heavy personal burden, and it hurts to tell it. It hurts more with each telling, as we the survivors know.

Now, here I was in business class, flying from Washington to Sydney, clutching a book recounting the story of the Obama presidency, relieved I had escaped the blizzard but, unbeknown to me, about to fly into a different kind of storm. A speech I had given months earlier and promptly forgotten had suddenly "gone viral."

Until now, I have never seen the speech written down. I delivered it unrehearsed and unscripted. I wanted it to be immediate and forceful. I wanted to look the audience in the eye and hold them. I didn't want to look down at notes. I didn't need them, for this story I had been told since childhood. It was a story I had reported on as a journalist in faraway countries, in which people felt the sting of invasion and colonisation. It was a "war story," and as the Vietnamese writer and academic Viet Thanh Nguyen, speaking of his own turbulent history, says: "All wars are fought twice, the first time on the battlefield, the second time in memory."

Obama's book *The Audacity of Hope* took America by storm and Stan's speech took this country by storm. This Australian Dream, the one he hopes for, and about which he argues with ghostly and real interlocutors, including his wife, is an audacious vision. If Australians are better than the cowards who booed Adam Goodes off the field, than the spiteful ordinary racists who make snide remarks about an irrelevant white bloodline, or about his success, then they need to know how Aboriginal men feel about the thousands of micro-aggressions against which they fight with all the psychological and linguistic power they can muster. I hope this essay is a slap-down for the racists and a cause for hope for those who believe, like Stan, that we can be better than this.

Marcia Langton

Kim Mahood

Stan Grant's Quarterly Essay speaks to the complexity of Indigenous identity in Australia today. It is easy to see why he has become a pin-up for the evolving conversation about Aboriginal identity and its place in Australian society. Subtle, passionate, judicious, generous – he holds white Australia to account, but does so without anger. Grant has been criticised for his willingness to give white Australians room to find a position where we are not all racist by default. Although he speaks with passion and depth about the suffering and disenfranchisement of his forebears, he doesn't scare or alienate white people. He makes it possible for us to hear him without the static of irreconcilable arguments. He also speaks frankly about having generations of white ancestry and how this has created an Indigenous identity very different from the deficit model of Aboriginality that dominates the media and the public perception. The history of his family, and others with a similar trajectory, is not so different from that of many white rural working-class families, except for the impact of the systemic racism enshrined in the law, embedded in the culture and present in the attitudes of even well-intentioned whites.

On reading the speech that prefaces the essay, and which I missed on its first outing, I took the sentence "The Australian Dream is rooted in racism" as a simple statement of fact, rather than an accusation. And taking it as a statement of fact made it easy to ask, "So how do we change it?", rather than feeling the need to qualify or deny it. There is something about the way Grant presents his argument that disarms resistance – the appeal to the highest common denominator rather than the lowest.

Grant tells the story of Aboriginal people who have jobs and mortgages and university degrees, who live in cities and large regional towns, who have middle-class lives and middle-class aspirations. In saying, "I want to challenge the politics of identity that can trap us in perpetual victimhood," he pre-empts the criticism levelled at Indigenous people by many white Australians, and challenges those who are complicit in the victim narrative. It marks a turning point, I think, when someone like Stan Grant stands up and says, "I am who and where I am in spite of the past, and now let's focus on the future."

While he gives history its due, and the historical overview he provides in the essay is compelling, he also suggests that to dwell on historical injustices is to remain trapped by them. To this argument he brings the insights wrung from a decade's experience covering conflicts in parts of the world where historical grudges are paid out in blood and hatred.

As someone who has benefited from the Australian Dream – indeed is among its highest achievers – not because he is Aboriginal, but because he is educated, intelligent, hard-working and ambitious, Grant is conscious of the irony of his position. But it took another high achiever, the formidable Marcia Langton, to set him on the course towards that ambition, to aim higher than he imagined was possible. And he goes on to remind us that, "If the Australian Dream is rooted in racism, then it has been the struggle of Indigenous people to rise above it ..." He attributes his own rise to the determination and courage of his parents and earlier generations to prevail in spite of racism, bigotry and legal discrimination.

While Grant cites his Wiradjuri and Kamilaroi ancestry as central to his identity, he does not claim a deep connection to country. Instead, he identifies the resilience of his forebears with their willingness to move. He presents the radical idea that it was through becoming migrants in other people's country in order to find work opportunities and engage in the white economy that his forebears transcended the obstacles stacked against them and carved out their place.

I found this story fascinating, telling as it does the experience of Aboriginal people whose lives were enmeshed with whites from the first days of colonisation. The first generation of "half-castes," thought to embody the worst characteristics of both races, were shuffled away to missions, educated with a view to producing a labour pool, and taught Christianity, which had the unintended consequence of providing them with a biblical model of exile and wandering.

This early fracturing of traditional connections to country, and the distinction between "half-caste" and "full-blood," produced an underclass that evolved to become people like Stan Grant's family, who felt that Australia did not have a place for them, and who did not think of themselves as Australian. One wonders, if there had been a word equivalent to the Canadian métis (derived from a French word meaning "mixed," apparently free of derogatory implications, and still in common use), whether the first generations of mixed-race people in Australia might have been able to establish a less-conflicted identity.

On several readings of the essay, what stays with me is the generational effect of the casual, quotidian racism that has been part of Australian culture since colonisation. This gives me renewed and greater respect for the Indigenous people who continue to rise above it, and some shame at judging unkindly those who display their wounds with less grace.

Inevitably, by focusing on the achievements of the predominantly urban Indigenous middle class – the quiet achievers who lead ordinary lives and the high achievers who contribute significantly to our sporting, cultural and intellectual life – Grant's project to shift the focus from the conventional view of Indigenous failure widens the gap between people like him and the people who provide the statistics for the deficit model.

He articulates his baffled discomfort at the sight of the drunks fighting in a park in Broome: "They are wiry and deeply black, with shocks of matted curly hair. They wear jeans stained with red dirt and checked polyester shirts; some have cowboy hats turned at the brim ... Two of the men stand and shape up. They swing wildly at each other ... No one intervenes ... Eventually a police van arrives; there is no urgency." His reaction is complicated by a sense that he should have some common cause with these "deeply black" fringe dwellers, that his own identity is enmeshed with theirs, although the gap that separates him from them is much greater than the gap between them and the white welfare class.

The majority of white Australians, who live in suburbs and cities, are more likely to encounter an Aboriginal person from the middle or professional class, and this is where I think the essay is a watershed, paving the way for a normalising of Indigenous identity. That this will happen at the cost of widening the gap between urban and remote Indigenous lives is one of those irreconcilable contradictions that make a mockery of rhetoric, good intentions and government policies.

Where I differ with Grant is in his charge that Jon Altman idealises Aboriginal people in remote communities, and with his take on Altman's comment, "I fail to see how standard education will assist those who live fundamentally non-standard lives." First, I doubt that Altman is an idealist – idealism doesn't survive thirty years of close encounters with remote Australia. It's more likely that he, like many others, has been drawn into a world of relationships and responsibilities that includes an understanding, difficult to articulate, that there is something of fundamental value in the evolving culture of remote Australia. To offer a different model is not necessarily to submit to the "soft bigotry of low expectations," but to aim for a kind of excellence that bridges different knowledge systems.

When the Northern Territory Intervention was imposed, a laconic white community manager remarked, "The prime minister seems to think that if you squeeze a blackfella tightly enough a whitefella will pop out." The graphic image this conjures up has stuck with me as a metaphor for government attitudes and policy towards remote Aboriginal Australia, along with a companion image of the squashed and resentful blackfella it actually produces.

The truth is that as long as people hold strongly to their country, their language and their traditions, they will live lives that differ in radical ways from most Australians. To shut down the communities (or to starve them out by stealth, which is the hidden agenda), and force people into towns which lack the resources, housing and jobs for them, will be to re-create the disaster of the earlier dispossessions, and to consign a large proportion of those people to the scrap heap. It is an intractable situation, and there are no easy solutions. The hybrid economy is happening, incrementally and with plenty of glitches along the way, but it is a real change and an important one.

The north is getting blacker, as more Aboriginal babies survive and people have more children. And while the remote communities are better places to live than the town fringe camps, and there is nothing in place to provide a viable alternative, it is better to work with reality than to bunker down behind rhetoric. The dramatic change in the Indigenous middle class, which is producing a visible and expanding professional class, is counterbalanced by the incremental generational change taking place in remote communities. The hybrid-economy model that Jon Altman and others are working towards is grounded in pragmatism, along with the recognition that it is a work in progress, subject to constant modifications.

Another development is the creative collaboration between artists, filmmakers and remote Indigenous people, which is producing radical and unique work. Given the pre-eminence of sporting ability, song, dance, film and art, why not build sporting and creative Centres for Excellence near the source – in Katherine, for instance, and Fitzroy Crossing and Laura. These small towns are located in some of the most spectacular landscapes in the country, and the remote communities are not remote if you are in Katherine or Laura; they are just down the unsealed, corrugated road. Invite the best practitioners and teachers, set rigorous standards, provide the best that both international and Indigenous cultures have to offer.

When describing the Indigenous people of previous generations who fought for equality and inclusion, Grant says, "these were people of resilience, pride, intelligence and dreams." Those qualities are harder to see among the rubbish and camp dogs and substance abuse and violence and truancy and diabetes and trachoma. But they are there, along with the subversiveness and humour and resourcefulness that have infiltrated the Australian character, if not the Australian Dream.

A few years ago I asked a mixed-race friend who lives on a remote community what she thought would produce lasting change in such communities.

"When there's more half-castes living in them," she replied.

If the deficit model of Aboriginality can be lifted from the urban Indigenous professional class, maybe some of its members will see their way clear to putting in time in remote communities, to bring their skills and insight to bear on what has so far proven beyond the capacity of white Australia.

Kim Mahood

Jon Altman

In *The Australian Dream* Stan Grant finds it baffling that I, as "an economist and anthropologist who has held a professorial post at the Australian National University," might be suggesting that an Aboriginal child would not benefit from, nor have the right to, the educational opportunities that I have enjoyed. I find this baffling too. Did I say that? I went back to examine Grant's source material in *Culture Crisis* and found I had said this:

> The fourth [explanator of the fundamental shift in Indigenous policy and practice in the twenty-first century] is a pervasive view drawn from human capital theory that postulates unproblematically that closing the education gap will improve socioeconomic outcomes, irrespective of cross-cultural or intercultural contexts or territorial spaces, a view that seems to be shared by Noel Pearson and Helen Hughes among others. I am no expert on education but I fail to see how standard education will assist those who live fundamentally non-standard lives.

This is very different from Grant's "He disavows the value of standard education for Indigenous children because they 'live fundamentally non-standard lives.'" I am not sure if this quote-mining is intended to set me up as a straw man to spice up Grant's essay, or if it is a genuine misunderstanding. Either way, if I ignore the misrepresentation of my views by Grant, I might stand accused of partaking in what Noel Pearson refers to as "the soft bigotry of low expectations."

Over the past forty years I have seen standard delivery of monolingual education, where the focus is more on attendance than performance, failing in many remote contexts. Even today, with draconian state intervention, attendance rates remain low, often hovering around the 50 to 60 per cent mark, despite parents being liable for financial penalty if their children do not turn up to school.

But I am not against education; rather, I champion the right of Aboriginal children to education, irrespective of where they live. As a foundation director of Karrkad-Kanjdji Trust, I am involved in a project to bring educational opportunity in the form of the Nawarddeken Academy to Kabulwarnamyo, an outstation in the Warddeken Indigenous Protected Area in remote West Arnhem Land. Here, students learn from teachers and parents, in English and their first language, Bininj Kunwok. The school is part of the community, and the community is part of the school. Attendance rates currently exceed 90 per cent.

I advocate for the rights of Aboriginal people to live remotely, to get an education and to receive services that support their choice of a future on their ancestral lands. I am helping garner philanthropic support to achieve this aim because of the current unwillingness of the Australian state to fund educational alterity, even when evidence shows it is working.

Does this make me, as Grant suggests, someone who "idealises Aboriginal people in remote communities living outside mainstream Australian life"? I do not think so.

In 1979 and 1980 I lived with a group of Kuninjku-speaking people in remote and difficult circumstances in Arnhem Land and documented how they were surviving living at outstations. What I found can only be described as an extraordinary transformation – people who had mainly lived as hunter-gatherers until 1963, the year Stan Grant was born, were now combining elements of their customary economy with engagement with market capitalism on their terms, mediated by a then sympathetic state willing to provide welfare entitlements and some rudimentary access to services. These people were living in a nonstandard way, but their circumstances were not, to use Grant's terms, "culturally 'pure.'" Kuninjku people had been thoroughly colonised by the Australian state, but they were nonetheless determined as a community to refashion postcolonial livelihood options for themselves living on land they owned under land rights law.

Living with these people for eighteen months left me with no illusions about the livelihood challenges they faced. Indeed, the information I collected showed that on average people worked the equivalent of full-time in self-provisioning and in production for market exchange. I used these data to challenge Marshall Sahlins's influential "original affluence" hypothesis, and made the point that if people have to work hard to survive today, it is likely they had to work much harder pre-colonially. Nothing idealistic here.

In 2001, after two decades of further research with Kuninjku people, I explained the transformation of their economic system using the notion of "economic hybridity." This theory is based on observed practice; it is not normative, nor predictive, nor prescriptive. It describes the way Kuninjku people struggle to creatively balance the customary and the market, as well as the dominant and now domineering state, assisted by their community-based organisations.

The tension between the demands of what the late anthropologist Bill Stanner termed in 1958 the Dreaming and the Market, between continuity and change, distils the challenge facing remote-living Indigenous people. Grant also uses partial quotation to misrepresent Stanner's view: Stanner's tentative "Indeed, there is a sense in which the Dreaming and the Market are mutually exclusive" becomes the definitive "The Dreaming and the Market are mutually exclusive."

Stanner and I are two white anthropologists who attract Grant's mild rebuke. This honourable link (for me) is a reminder of research I undertook a decade ago about Stanner as a policy intellectual. His disciplinary background, like mine, was in economics and anthropology, and, like Grant, he had earlier worked as a journalist. Much of his policy work focused on the problems associated with disadvantage and the need to reduce the disparity between Aboriginal and other Australians. At the same time, his sympathetic cultural analysis indicated that this difference could be viewed as a social good in a plural, multicultural Australia. Stanner was comfortable with socio-economic sameness and assimilation as long as this was predicated on choice made by Aboriginal people. And so am I. But in my research I see options to live differently being rapidly diminished by an increasingly intolerant, paternalistic and intrusive state practising what William Davies has recently termed "punitive neoliberalism."

I note that while Stan Grant is critical of my hybrid-economy formulation, he is comfortable with its deployment by my colleagues Ian Keen and Chris Lloyd in their important revisionist economic history project *Indigenous Participation in Australian Economies*. In the nineteenth century, hybrid economic formations did emerge out of violent conflict between groups like Grant's forebears the Wiradjuri and ruthless land-grabbing white invaders. Today the form of economic violence might be different, but the diverse responses of Indigenous groups that have resulted in economic plurality are no less heroic.

And looking to the future, Grant is again comfortable with hybridity – he lauds the leadership of Indigenous people like Northern Land Council CEO and my long-term colleague Joe Morrison, in "trying to chart a course between economic engagement and maintaining distinct and different cultural and value systems: how to stay black and prosper." Grant does not seem to realise how the course he approves aligns closely with the hybrid-economy formulation.

Today 3.3 million square kilometres, 43 per cent of the Australian continent, is held under some form of Indigenous title. On these lands Indigenous people enjoy native title rights, most evident in the right to use wildlife for household consumption. Many Indigenous people have fought hard to prove their continuity of custom and tradition and ongoing connection to land that was illegally appropriated. Having done so, they now want to reside on these lands and enjoy a decent livelihood.

Hence, when I ask Kuninjku people what constitutes "the good life" for them, it is about maintaining close relations with kin, country – where the old people are buried – sacred sites and ceremony, and access to bush foods. Migration for education or employment is something they would not countenance.

In situations where people will not migrate, I restate what I wrote a decade ago on education: too much emphasis is being placed on providing opportunity for Indigenous kids in remote Australia for imagined futures as "lawyers, doctors and plumbers" (to use the words of Amanda Vanstone); and too little emphasis is placed on futures as artists, land managers, hunters and now carbon farmers living on the land they own. Rather than just seek mainstream education solutions to complex, non-mainstream Indigenous circumstances, we should develop appropriate curricula – as is occurring at the Nawarddeken Academy – relevant to local settings, and innovative local enterprises.

Grant takes issue with my concern that it is risky to "close the gap" by forcing people into the mainstream capitalist economy. Today the Community Development Programme (CDP) seeks to deliver the impossible goal of employment parity for 35,000 unemployed adults in regional and remote Australia. This so-called employment program is imposed on groups as diverse as Grant's Wiradjuri of western New South Wales and the Kuninjku of western Arnhem Land. It requires able-bodied people to work five hours a day, five days a week, year round, in work-like activity that is referred to by some participants as "bullshit jobs," at pay well below the basic award.

In 2015–16, the first year of CDP, only 2760 participants held a job for six months. It is not clear what the jobs were and if the participants were Indigenous. There are 60 CDP regions, so that means an average of forty-five six-month outcomes per region. Such low numbers are not surprising, as jobs are very hard to come by in remote Australia. In the same year there were 146,654 financial penalties levied on 20,409 participants. About 90 per cent of those penalised were Indigenous. Each penalty "event" costs participants a minimum of $50, or one-tenth of their fortnightly welfare payment.

These facts indicate that CDP and its surveillance system is much more efficient in penalising participants than finding them jobs; participation requirements are too onerous and unfair, exceeding those in more settled regions, and remote jobs too scarce. So I stand by my concern, now verified by official statistics, about the unacceptable risk that is further entrenching Indigenous poverty in regional and remote Australia, a dire situation that Grant chooses to overlook in his essay.

Stan Grant tells a compelling autobiographical story of his economic and geographic migration, of a form of rugged individualism that has not only garnered him socio-economic success, but has also allowed him to retain a layered identity inclusive of his Wiradjuri ancestry. He misconstrues his status – he is not a member of an emerging Indigenous middle class, but a member of a small Indigenous elite that has significant influence with the most powerful political, bureaucratic and corporate actors in Australia. With such status comes both responsibility and accountability, especially when, as a public intellectual, he is promoting approaches informed by his own lived experience. Autobiography is not a sound basis for policy-making; and identity politics needs to be clearly differentiated from the realpolitik of ongoing settler-colonial creative destruction.

The challenge that I try to address in my work is what development alternatives are we as a nation providing to those whose Australian Dream is to live fundamentally differently and remotely? I have no definitive answer, but my observations over decades point to some promising possibilities that fuse elements of hybrid economic forms and self-determination. These possibilities are currently being extinguished in the name of economic sameness – a sameness that Stan Grant seems to condone.

Jon Altman

Nicholas Biddle

Stan Grant's Quarterly Essay comes at an interesting time in Indigenous affairs policy. This is a period of policy experimentation that is in many ways quite radical, with trials of a cashless welfare card (in Ceduna, South Australia and the Kimberley, Western Australia); the tying of welfare payments to school enrolment and attendance (in the Northern Territory); and the use of "direct instruction" and a "back-to-basics" approach to schooling (in Cape York, Queensland). There has also been continuous change in employment services in remote Australia, with the introduction of the Community Development Programme, replacing the Remote Jobs and Communities Program. The community development component of the more recent program is arguably in name only.

These are just a few of the high-level policy changes. There is also much experimentation occurring at the state and territory government level (Local Decision Making in New South Wales, Regional Partnerships in South Australia and Treaty negotiations in a number of jurisdictions), as well as at the local or community level.

Within this context, what is immediately interesting about Grant's essay is the strength and diversity of the Indigenous voices he quotes. Warren Mundine, Noel Pearson, Marcia Langton, Joe Morrison, Yin Paradies and Kerryn Pholi are a few of the high-profile and emerging authors and thinkers he engages with (alongside many non-Indigenous authors). There is clearly heated debate going on within Indigenous Australia, and the essay gives the rest of us a window onto this.

The Australian Dream has two quite simple but powerful messages. First, that Indigenous identity is complex and multilayered, and interacts with other identities that need not be mutually exclusive. Second, that for many Indigenous Australians, success within the mainstream economy is both desirable and achievable, but that this often occurs alongside and can be a result of a form of "economic migration." These messages are conveyed in a typically engaging way, with Grant weaving in his own family history, the words and thoughts of some of the thinkers mentioned above, and statistics and research findings. It is on this last point that I want to make a few comments.

Grant states that, "65 per cent of Indigenous people in Australia (360,000) are employed and living lives, materially and socio-economically, like those of other Australians." This is sourced from a Centre for Independent Studies report. But it is a very long way off the true figure. Our best and most recent estimate is that only around 204,000 Indigenous Australians were employed in 2014–15, of whom around 81,000 were employed part-time. When you look at the working-age Indigenous population (15 to 64 years), only 48.3 per cent were employed.

This isn't a criticism of the essay – we are all reliant on material in the public domain. It also doesn't detract from Grant's main point, that there are many Indigenous Australians who are doing very well, that they are doing so despite the historical injustices they have experienced, and that there is much we as a country could learn from and should admire in their success. But scale does matter, and it is important to be accurate in how we report this success. More than half of the working-age Indigenous population are not working, compared to only a little over a quarter (26.1 per cent) of the total Australian population. Clearly the historical injustice and the ongoing discrimination that Grant talks about so eloquently goes deeper than we as a country should be satisfied with, or the statistics from the Centre for Independent Studies would suggest.

Grant sees employment in the mainstream economy as the clearest way for Indigenous peoples to participate in modern Australian society on equal terms. There is much justification for this: Grant talks about many Indigenous men and women who have found that relocating to urban areas opens doors to employment. However, if this is the case, we must recognise that movement from remote to non-remote areas and economic migration in general also comes with social and economic costs that must be weighed against the benefits.

Some of these costs have historically been hidden, due to lack of data. However, drawing on a new census dataset, analysis by myself and colleagues at the ANU showed that a non-employed Indigenous Australian who moved from a remote to a non-remote area was in fact less likely to be employed five years later than an otherwise identical Indigenous Australian who stayed in remote Australia over the same period (2006 to 2011).

That is, moving out of a remote area appears to make employment less, not more, likely. This is perhaps unsurprising. If someone moves away from their home, they lose access to local networks (from which many of us obtain employment) and must compete in very different labour markets with different skills distributions. And we know that labour-market discrimination is higher in non-remote than remote areas.

That is not to say that employment outcomes wouldn't eventually improve. Or that there aren't other benefits for those who do move and their families (the intergenerational advantages Grant talks about). But we can't ignore the costs of economic migration.

The recurring theme of Grant's essay is identity. Grant writes of the multiple and competing identities that all of us have, but which are particularly salient for many Indigenous Australians. As a non-Indigenous researcher who has tried to build statistical models of Indigenous population change, the insights from Grant's story and that of his family are both moving and revelatory.

Some additional data from the census can, however, be added to the story. Specifically, when we link censuses across years, we can see that Indigenous identification is highly context-specific and much more variable than once thought. While it is true that in net terms more people are changing their identification from non-Indigenous to Indigenous than the other way around, changes from Indigenous to non-Indigenous aren't insignificant. More than one in ten people who were identified as Indigenous in 2006 did not lay claim to the same identity in 2011. This might be because in one year they filled out the form themselves, but in other years someone else in the household did. Either way, not only is identity layered and complex, how it is revealed to data collectors, and hence policy-makers, is highly variable.

Ultimately, *The Australian Dream* is a powerful essay on Australia's first peoples and their place in Australian society. It busts many myths and highlights the diversity of the Indigenous population, when we are all too often only shown the disadvantage and the damage of history. It should be required reading for all those who want to understand why policy in this area has so often failed, and how it might be done better.

Nicholas Biddle

THE AUSTRALIAN DREAM

Stan Grant

"*Homo sum, humani nihil a me alienum puto* — I am human, and nothing that is human is alien to me."

The playwright Terence — a man bought and sold as a slave in ancient Rome — penned those words, which speak to me still today.

That quote inspired my essay. I sought to look beyond the parochial aspects of identity, to look to those things that inform our shared humanity. I am a liberal cosmopolitan — someone who prefers a layered identity rather than an essentialist, fundamentalist self-conception that sets me apart from others.

The textured fabric of difference that enriches our lives should be cherished. I am blessed to have been born into a family deeply connected to its Indigenous heritage; a family of love and laughter and story which sustains me still. Yet I am the sum of many parts. My family is drawn from the mixed-race (so-called "half-caste") people of the Australian frontier. Our lives were shaped by our whiteness and our blackness. We carry the names of white settlers — in my case an Irish rebel convict. I have a white grandmother on my mother's side, someone who was dear to me and whom I would never seek to deny.

Kim Mahood, in her reply to my essay, makes a very salient point, wondering whether, if there had been a word equivalent to the Canadian métis (mixed), this might have allowed for the development of a less-conflicted identity. Certainly I believe such a term would be more accurate. The history of the people I am drawn from is unique, and we lose much of the richness and nuance when it is described as generically Indigenous.

Australian officialdom has turned itself inside out trying to classify people who don't fit easily into an explicit category. The Australian Law Reform Commission has counted sixty-four separate definitions of "Aboriginal." Among Indigenous people — particularly in my case in New South Wales — "colour" has always been a sensitive and defining characteristic. As my essay shows, in the mid-twentieth-century assimilation era a social hierarchy developed, which placed lighter-skinned Aboriginal people above their darker cousins. There were economic consequences, as those deemed more likely to be absorbed into the general population gained houses in town, employment and better education for their children.

My essay quotes the work of the anthropologist Ruth Fink, who surveyed one western NSW town and found that many Aborigines considered themselves superior to others because they were married to a white person. The demographer and historian Charles Rowley talks of a "two-tiered" Aboriginal society. Some Aboriginal people demanded the right to be classified as "white," with the rights this entailed.

The academic and Indigenous woman Maria Lane followed the trail of many Aboriginal people as they moved from missions and settlements to towns and cities. They were the pioneer economic migrants who seized on social and economic mobility. She found their grandchildren excelling at school and university. She dubbed these people the "open society" – diverse, racially mixed, they were married to non-Indigenous people, and were risk- and reward-oriented, resisting government intervention in their lives. They were still self-identifying as "Indigenous," with links to community and kin, but were rejecting orthodox notions of "Aboriginality" and reimagining themselves in more sophisticated and complex ways.

This has been the story of my family. We have always identified, and been defined variously, as "Aboriginal." Like other families, we have been shaped by government policies of exclusion and segregation. These policies told us where we could live, whom we could marry and whether we could keep our children. My family, like so many Aboriginal families, suffered enormously. I was born into this legacy of poverty and bigotry.

In a very real sense my struggle has been to reconcile not just the history of this country, but the very blood in my veins. George Megalogenis identifies this dilemma that sits at the very heart of our nation. Australia, for much of its history, sought to deny its own inheritance. How many white families are oblivious to their black past?

My essay traces what I believe is a far too neglected story, of those people classified as Aboriginal who looked for a way into a country that had rejected and excluded them. It is not a denial – as Amy McQuire has tried to argue – of the wrongs of our past. I explicitly pointed out that I did not want my essay to be another tale of woe, yet I could not and did not ignore the plight of those who suffer the most: that is unquestionably linked to the legacy of history. My essay contained the caveat that much of that story has been told, and I noted significant work by Indigenous and non-Indigenous people that has punctured what anthropologist W.E.H. Stanner called "The Great Australian Silence."

However, there is another story. It is a story that begins on the Australian frontier with Aboriginal people engaging with the growing economy. The records are replete with examples of Indigenous cooperatives and farming ventures. The colonial administrators saw missions in part as places of training, and, indeed, many children were schooled there, learning to read and write proficiently.

In the twentieth century a generation of leaders emerged: educated, courageous and determined to find a place in Australia. These were people who saw themselves as the inheritors of the traditions of their Aboriginal forebears and their white ancestry. William Cooper – one of the leading voices of the 1930s – saw his people as "Black Britishers." They demanded citizenship and equality, they fought to end segregation and they fought in our country's wars.

These weren't dupes or supplicants. They weren't abandoning "the mob" – they were transforming their lives and inspiring their people. They looked for work, travelled long distances and uprooted their families. I make the point that they were "economic migrants." I concede this is a challenging concept for Indigenous people, but like migrants the world over they hoped for a better life and they exercised their own agency. Were they exploited? Yes. Just like migrants historically everywhere. Were we discriminated against? Yes. Yet we have succeeded despite that. In so doing, our people changed this country.

My essay is unapologetically focused on individuals. These people are the vanguard of the emerging Indigenous middle class. Melbourne University's Professor Marcia Langton has dubbed this a "quiet revolution." Dr Julie Lahn from the Australian National University says the rise of Aboriginal university-educated professionals living and working in urban Australia has been overlooked, impeding understanding of the transformation of Indigenous society itself. Education has been critical. In twenty years the number of Indigenous graduates of universities grew from fewer than 4000 to more than 30,000. They include people like Sana Nakata, a mixed-heritage Torres Strait Islander following her father as a second-generation Indigenous PhD. She is typical of the new breed, not wishing to be celebrated solely as an Indigenous person but as a professional in her own right.

McQuire is sceptical – even dismissive – of this individual success. She claims this "Australian Dream" is a world away from the aspirations of Aboriginal people. She accuses me of proffering a very limited view of black success. This is typically myopic, framing authenticity around a narrow definition of presumed collective or communal identity. There is an orthodoxy – dare

I say a fundamentalism – here that is debilitating. It is what academic and Indigenous man Yin Paradies calls a "prison-house identity" that stifles any attempt at a more layered or hybrid sense of self. Paradies says there is a deep hostility in sections of the Indigenous community towards people like himself. He has been labelled a "coconut" – brown on the outside, white on the inside. It is a common insult.

It is common to see self-appointed "identity police" acting as arbiters of who is or is not Indigenous. It is often associated with lateral violence; intimidation and harsh judgment that I have seen inflict enormous harm on vulnerable people. I prefer a much more expansive view of Aboriginal people. I reject a definition of Aboriginality predicated on community endorsement. This does not mean I don't value my deep community connections. Successful people have the freedom of choice and options, and we can live comfortably in distinct or overlapping milieus.

McQuire says my notion of success is tied to my own journey and identity. Indeed, I have pursued an individual career – I wanted to be the best journalist I could be and to work in the world's most fascinating places. I have never accepted that being Indigenous meant I could not equally be fascinated by Chinese history, Russian politics or the crises of the Middle East. My life has been enriched by living in different countries, learning new languages and experiencing diverse cultures. I have precious friendships with people of many nationalities, built on our shared humanity. Honing my skills, winning the respect of my peers, has also meant I can bring that journalistic expertise to telling the stories of Indigenous Australia.

Yes, I have worked for the ABC, CNN and Channel 7, but I made my first on-air appearance as a nervous student on an Aboriginal community radio program in Canberra. My aunt was instrumental in getting Indigenous voices heard. When I returned to Australia after more than a decade overseas, I worked for National Indigenous Television, heading the coverage of the network's free-to-air launch, establishing the current affairs programs Awaken and The Point and, I hope, helping to nurture and mentor a generation of young reporters.

I have a community among the Wiradjuri people of New South Wales; my family's ties run deep. I have responsibilities to that community and return home regularly to be among the people who mean the most to me. Pursuing my career, making my choices, has never meant turning away from – or being excluded by – people I consider my own. In my family are plumbers and doctors and teachers and labourers and public servants and military officers. Some have done very well; others have struggled. Most live still on our ancestral land; my father is a member of the Wiradjuri Council of Elders and a speaker and teacher of Wiradjuri language. We move freely and comfortably in our world, we contribute to our communities and we pursue our ambitions and dreams.

The great majority of people who identify as Indigenous are of mixed heritage. We live in urban centres, and many – as I do – have non-Indigenous partners. We are lacerated by class, gender and geography; all these factors shape our life prospects and our identities. We are connected to the history of dispossession, suffering and injustice. Yet, as my essay argues, history need not be destiny. Notions of Indigenous identity rely heavily on a historical narrative based on memory. It can be fraught and fragile. As the French historian Jacques Le Goff says, "Memory only seeks to rescue the past in order to serve the present and the future."

Identity rooted in a sense of unending and irresolvable grievance does not aid reconciliation. The writer David Rieff warns of the perils of relying on historical memory; it is selective and unreliable. He reminds us that it sits at the heart of so many of the world's intractable and bloody disputes: Hutu and Tutsi, Shi'a and Sunni, Hindu and Muslim, Catholic and Protestant. Amartya Sen says "solitarist identities" based on opposition and difference breed violence. Sen says they savagely challenge our shared humanity and ultimately make the world flammable. In a thirty-year career reporting the world's flashpoints, I have seen this time and again. My challenge as an Indigenous person is how to remember the past without being its victim.

Australia, like all nations, is an ongoing project. I concede that throughout my life I have struggled with the notion of allegiance to a country that for so long excluded my forebears. Yet I find myself today by any measure enjoying great privilege. Australia in 2017 is a country where nearly a third of the landmass is held under some form of title by Indigenous groups. The Mabo case exposed the fiction of terra nullius. There is greater Indigenous representation in our parliaments. Taxpayers contribute upwards of $30 billion – directly or indirectly – towards Indigenous programs. There is widespread goodwill and support politically and among the general population. This does not mean there is not unresolved historical injustice, or that there are not still huge areas of suffering and policy failure. There are questions of treaty and recognition that may well lead to improved outcomes, and politically there are significant steps being taken towards that end. Australia today is not the country of 1788, nor is it 1901 or 1967; we cannot overlook progress, just as we cannot ignore the enormous remaining challenges.

The areas of greatest need are undoubtedly in the most isolated and remote parts of the country. This is where we see the entrenched poverty, domestic violence, drug and alcohol abuse, and high rates of imprisonment. In my essay I concede a lack of first-hand experience and knowledge of these communities. I admit that I don't necessarily share a cultural or social identity with these Indigenous people. We share links to common heritage but are shaped by different historical and economic factors. If I visit those communities, I am an outsider, if not a stranger.

Jon Altman has spent considerable time living among these people. In my essay I note that he correctly identifies the complexity of these remote communities. He suggests a hybrid economic solution built around some market exchange, customary activity and state support. He argues this offers a more socially secure future than the alternative of a more precarious position in the general economy. I concede there may be virtue in this, but it is inevitably limited. The anthropologist Nicolas Peterson looks at the outstation movements – people relocating to traditional country – as an example of what he calls "Indigenous life projects." It may lead to more autonomy, but he points out that it also means acceptance of a lower standard of living. To close the gap, he says, work – selling labour – will be the lot of most Aboriginal people, as it is for all Australians.

Altman's model does not speak to my experience or to the lived reality of the vast majority of people who identify as Indigenous. The biggest Aboriginal population in Australia is in western Sydney and there is no prospect of a "hybrid economy" there. We live in a fast-moving globalised world and our challenge is to find a secure place in it. The history of my people of south-eastern Australia has been one of social and economic engagement, in the face of generations of exclusion and discrimination. I am here because of their courage, sacrifice and resilience. Altman says that autobiography is not a basis for good policy. That is ridiculous. It should be essential to policy – real, lived outcomes, and initiatives that have made a measurable and enduring difference, should inform everything government does.

So, what works? Access to opportunity, proximity to infrastructure, adaptability, willingness to take a risk. Employment and education are crucial. In the prime minister's annual Closing the Gap speech in February, there was a ray of light amid the gloom: Indigenous people with a university degree have the same employment outcomes as non-Indigenous Australians. The 30,000-plus Indigenous graduates have closed the gap. They far outnumber the roughly 10,000 Aboriginal people in prison. It doesn't diminish the urgency of the plight of those behind bars – a horrendous statistical disparity – to acknowledge Indigenous success.

On the day of the speech, a range of confident, supremely educated, successful Indigenous people appeared in the media. Every one of them enjoys a privileged life. They are living proof that being Indigenous need not mean being trapped in unrelenting poverty. Professor Reuben Bolt from the University of New South Wales — an Indigenous man from the NSW south coast — said the political narrative needs to change. He rejects the language of disadvantage, instead arguing that Aboriginal people have historically been marginalised. It is a revealing distinction. My essay seeks to portray Indigenous efforts to overcome that marginality.

Where Aboriginal people engage with mainstream Australia, they can be enormously successful. There is a long history of what I have termed Indigenous "economic migrants" who have not only sought to transform their lives, but have also laid a foundation for the success of their descendants. The rise of the Aboriginal middle class is raising urgent — undoubtedly uncomfortable — questions about the nature of identity, culture and community. Like many, I demand the right to define myself. Appropriating others' suffering to bolster authenticity is offensive. I have no need of a vicarious identity framed around unending grievance and intractable poverty. I have many layers to my identity — none of them exclusive.

My Wiradjuri grandfather read the Bible and Shakespeare. His son — my father — has helped revive the language of his ancestors. I have been to Ireland and felt a bond with my Irish convict forebear. I am born out of the unique story of Australia — its triumphs and its shame. I am a person who seeks to find his place in the world and there are many Indigenous people who seek the same.

In the words of Terence: I am human, nothing that is human is alien to me.

Stan Grant

Jon Altman is a research professor in anthropology at Deakin University and an emeritus professor of the Australian National University.

Nicholas Biddle is an associate professor at the Centre for Aboriginal Economic Policy Research at the Australian National University.

Stan Grant is Indigenous affairs editor at the ABC and Chair of Indigenous Affairs at Charles Sturt University. He won the 2015 Walkley Award for coverage of Indigenous affairs and is the author of *The Tears of Strangers* and *Talking to My Country*.

Marcia Langton is professor of Australian Indigenous studies at the University of Melbourne. Her books include *The Quiet Revolution*, *Well, I heard it on the radio and I saw it on the television* and, as co-editor, *First Australians: An Illustrated History*.

Kim Mahood is the author of two books, *Position Doubtful* and *Craft for a Dry Lake*, and many essays for art, literary and current affairs journals.

David Marr is the author of *Patrick White: A Life*, *Panic*, *The High Price of Heaven* and *Dark Victory* (with Marian Wilkinson). He has written for the *Sydney Morning Herald*, the *Age*, the *Saturday Paper*, the *Guardian* and the *Monthly*, been editor of the *National Times*, a reporter for *Four Corners* and presenter of ABC TV's *Media Watch*. He is the author of five previous bestselling Quarterly Essays.

Amy McQuire is a Darumbal and South Sea Islander woman. A former editor of the *National Indigenous Times* and *Tracker* magazine, she writes for *New Matilda*, the *Monthly* online and the *Guardian*.

George Megalogenis's book *The Australian Moment* won the 2013 Prime Minister's Award for non-fiction and formed the basis for his ABC TV series *Making Australia Great*. His most recent book is *Australia's Second Chance*. He is the author of two Quarterly Essays, *Balancing Act* and *Trivial Pursuit*, recently re-published in a single book.

Jacinta Nampijinpa Price is a Warlpiri/Celtic woman, an Alice Springs town councillor and the founder of Yangapi Productions. For many years she has advocated against domestic violence and worked to empower Indigenous girls, women and children.

QUARTERLY ESSAY AUTO-RENEWING SUBSCRIPTIONS NOW AVAILABLE
SUBSCRIBE to Quarterly Essay & SAVE up to 23% on the cover price.

Enjoy free home delivery of the print edition and full digital access on the Quarterly Essay website, iPad, iPhone and Android apps.

FORTHCOMING ISSUES:

**Anna Krien on the Climate Deadlock
June 2017**

**Benjamin Law on Sexuality, Schools and the Media
September 2017**

....

Subscriptions: Receive a discount and never miss an issue. Mailed direct to your door.

☐ **1 year auto-renewing print and digital subscription*** (4 issues): $69.95 within Australia. Outside Australia $109.95

☐ **1 year print and digital subscription** (4 issues): $79.95 within Australia. Outside Australia $119.95

☐ **1 year auto-renewing digital subscription*** (4 issues): $34.95

☐ **1 year digital only subscription** (4 issues): $39.95

☐ **2 year print and digital subscription** (8 issues): $149.95 within Australia

Gift Subscriptions: Give an inspired gift.

☐ **1 year print and digital gift subscription** (4 issues): $79.95 within Australia. Outside Australia $119.95

☐ **1 year digital only gift subscription** (4 issues): $39.95

☐ **2 year print and digital gift subscription** (8 issues): $149.95 within Australia

All prices include GST, postage and handling. *Your subscription will automatically renew until you notify us to stop. Prior to the end of your subscription period, we will send you a reminder notice.

Please turn over for subscription order form, or subscribe online at **www.quarterlyessay.com**
Alternatively, call 1800 077 514 or 03 9486 0244 or email subscribe@blackincbooks.com

Back Issues: (Prices include GST, postage and handling.)

- ☐ **QE 1** ($15.99) Robert Manne *In Denial*
- ☐ **QE 2** ($15.99) John Birmingham *Appeasing Jakarta*
- ☐ **QE 3** ($15.99) Guy Rundle *The Opportunist*
- ☐ **QE 4** ($15.99) Don Watson *Rabbit Syndrome*
- ☐ **QE 4** ($15.99) Mungo MacCallum *Girt By Sea*
- ☐ **QE 6** ($15.99) John Button *Beyond Belief*
- ☐ **QE 7** ($15.99) John Martinkus *Paradise Betrayed*
- ☐ **QE 8** ($15.99) Amanda Lohrey *Groundswell*
- ☐ **QE 9** ($15.99) Tim Flannery *Beautiful Lies*
- ☐ **QE 10** ($15.99) Gideon Haigh *Bad Company*
- ☐ **QE 11** ($15.99) Germaine Greer *Whitefella Jump Up*
- ☐ **QE 12** ($15.99) David Malouf *Made in England*
- ☐ **QE 13** ($15.99) Robert Manne with David Corlett *Sending Them Home*
- ☐ **QE 14** ($15.99) Paul McGeough *Mission Impossible*
- ☐ **QE 15** ($15.99) Margaret Simons *Latham's World*
- ☐ **QE 16** ($15.99) Raimond Gaita *Breach of Trust*
- ☐ **QE 17** ($15.99) John Hirst *'Kangaroo Court'*
- ☐ **QE 18** ($15.99) Gail Bell *The Worried Well*
- ☐ **QE 19** ($15.99) Judith Brett *Relaxed & Comfortable*
- ☐ **QE 20** ($15.99) John Birmingham *A Time for War*
- ☐ **QE 21** ($15.99) Clive Hamilton *What's Left?*
- ☐ **QE 22** ($15.99) Amanda Lohrey *Voting for Jesus*
- ☐ **QE 23** ($15.99) Inga Clendinnen *The History Question*
- ☐ **QE 24** ($15.99) Robyn Davidson *No Fixed Address*
- ☐ **QE 25** ($15.99) Peter Hartcher *Bipolar Nation*
- ☐ **QE 26** ($15.99) David Marr *His Master's Voice*
- ☐ **QE 27** ($15.99) Ian Lowe *Reaction Time*
- ☐ **QE 28** ($15.99) Judith Brett *Exit Right*
- ☐ **QE 29** ($15.99) Anne Manne *Love & Money*
- ☐ **QE 30** ($15.99) Paul Toohey *Last Drinks*
- ☐ **QE 31** ($15.99) Tim Flannery *Now or Never*
- ☐ **QE 32** ($15.99) Kate Jennings *American Revolution*
- ☐ **QE 33** ($15.99) Guy Pearse *Quarry Vision*
- ☐ **QE 34** ($15.99) Annabel Crabb *Stop at Nothing*
- ☐ **QE 35** ($15.99) Noel Pearson *Radical Hope*
- ☐ **QE 36** ($15.99) Mungo MacCallum *Australian Story*
- ☐ **QE 37** ($15.99) Waleed Aly *What's Right?*
- ☐ **QE 38** ($15.99) David Marr *Power Trip*
- ☐ **QE 39** ($15.99) Hugh White *Power Shift*
- ☐ **QE 40** ($15.99) George Megalogenis *Trivial Pursuit*
- ☐ **QE 41** ($15.99) David Malouf *The Happy Life*
- ☐ **QE 42** ($15.99) Judith Brett *Fair Share*
- ☐ **QE 43** ($15.99) Robert Manne *Bad News*
- ☐ **QE 44** ($15.99) Andrew Charlton *Man-Made World*
- ☐ **QE 45** ($15.99) Anna Krien *Us and Them*
- ☐ **QE 46** ($15.99) Laura Tingle *Great Expectations*
- ☐ **QE 47** ($15.99) David Marr *Political Animal*
- ☐ **QE 48** ($15.99) Tim Flannery *After the Future*
- ☐ **QE 49** ($15.99) Mark Latham *Not Dead Yet*
- ☐ **QE 50** ($15.99) Anna Goldsworthy *Unfinished Business*
- ☐ **QE 51** ($15.99) David Marr *The Prince*
- ☐ **QE 52** ($15.99) Linda Jaivin *Found in Translation*
- ☐ **QE 53** ($15.99) Paul Toohey *That Sinking Feeling*
- ☐ **QE 54** ($15.99) Andrew Charlton *Dragon's Tail*
- ☐ **QE 55** ($15.99) Noel Pearson *A Rightful Place*
- ☐ **QE 56** ($15.99) Guy Rundle *Clivosaurus*
- ☐ **QE 57** ($15.99) Karen Hitchcock *Dear Life*
- ☐ **QE 58** ($22.99) David Kilcullen *Blood Year*
- ☐ **QE 59** ($22.99) David Marr *Faction Man*
- ☐ **QE 60** ($22.99) Laura Tingle *Political Amnesia*
- ☐ **QE 61** ($22.99) George Megalogenis *Balancing Act*
- ☐ **QE 62** ($22.99) James Brown *Firing Line*
- ☐ **QE 63** ($22.99) Don Watson *Enemy Within*
- ☐ **QE 64** ($22.99) Stan Grant *The Australian Dream*

☐ I enclose a cheque/money order made out to Schwartz Publishing Pty Ltd.

☐ Please debit my credit card (Mastercard, Visa or Amex accepted).

Card No. ☐☐☐☐ ☐☐☐☐ ☐☐☐☐ ☐☐☐☐

Expiry date   /   **CCV**   **Amount $**

Cardholder's name   **Signature**

Name

Address

Email   **Phone**

Post or fax this form to: Quarterly Essay, Reply Paid 90094, Carlton VIC 3053 / Freecall: 1800 077 514
Tel: (03) 9486 0288 / Fax: (03) 9011 6106 / Email: subscribe@quarterlyessay.com
Subscribe online at **www.quarterlyessay.com**